Political Action

political action

a practical guide to movement politics

michael walzer

chicago
Quadrangle Books

POLITICAL ACTION. Copyright © 1971 by Michael Walzer. All rights reserved, including the right to reproduce this book or portions thereof in any form. For information, address: Quadrangle Books, Inc., 12 East Delaware Place, Chicago 60611. Manufactured in the United States of America. Published simultaneously in Canada by Burns and MacEachern Ltd., Toronto.

Library of Congress Catalog Card: 79–143571
SBN Cloth 8129–0173–8
SBN Paper 8129–6142–0

for Sarah and Rebecca
whether they choose to be activists
or not

Foreword

Michael Walzer has written a discerning and useful guide
for political participation. At a time when much political
commentary is either apocalyptic or cynical or purely
pragmatic without concern for principle, it is a pleasure to
come upon a book which reflects a sense of idealism along
with a sense of strategy. The author has been involved in what
is called "the movement" and also in various electoral
campaigns. He has learned from these experiences. And
mixing experience and thoughtful reflection in his book, he
recommends a broad range of possible political activities.
Although his readers will not be assured of victory if they
follow his prescriptions, they will, I think, be saved from many
political follies and be helped along the way to success.
Mr. Walzer is a political activist and a political philosopher.
The tension between the two, as well as that between ends and
means, purposes and tactics, is reflected in his book as
it should be, since these tensions are part of every political
effort. Mr. Walzer makes his point without elaborate or what in
many cases are misleading statistical devices. The book is
written with lucidity and with wit. It is my hope that *Political
Action* will be widely read. If it is, the politics of the country,
as we move toward 1972 and beyond, will be better as to
its purposes and more effective in its methods.

Eugene McCarthy

Preface

I wrote most of this little book in the weeks immediately following the American invasion of Cambodia, almost a year ago. It is a political response to that event and to the outburst of citizen activism that followed. I want to emphasize that it is far more the work of an amateur activist than of a professional political scientist. I cannot claim much detachment from the people whose politics is described and (often) criticized in these pages. The criticisms are ones I have actually made or listened to other people make at meetings, and I have not hesitated to reproduce the hope, the anger, the weariness that my friends and I—and doubtless our opponents too—felt at such moments. It is my purpose to recommend political action of a certain sort, not political action in general, to my readers. The best way to do that, it seems to me, is simply to join the debates that go on every day in citizens' clubs and movements.

I have encountered one difficulty that ought to be mentioned here. There is no classical history of citizen politics to which I can refer. Even movements of national scope are too little known in their details to serve as easy references. In any case, my own experience is with local activism, of little interest except to fellow participants in this or that project. So I have often failed to be concrete, though many readers will surely be able to supplement my advice with experiences that will serve (I hope) to confirm it.

Citizen politics is not an affair of lonely leaders or abstracted theorists. It is a roughly equalitarian and highly sociable activity, and one gets along, if at all, with a lot of help from one's friends. I have had help writing this book, most especially from Carolyn Grace, Irving Howe, Martin Peretz, and Judith Walzer, comrades in different enterprises.

M. W.

January 1971

Contents

Foreword by Eugene McCarthy 7

Preface 9

1 The Political Moment 15

2 Beginnings 20

3 Strategic Choices 23

4 Defining the Issues 28

5 Searching for a Constituency 32

6 Going to the People 36

7 Coalitions 39

8 Political Geography 44

9 Three Organizational Structures 48

10 Leaders 55

11 Raising and Spending Money 60

12 The Woman Question 65

13 Meetings 68

14 The Office Staff 73

15 Personal Relations in the Movement 75

16 Quackery and Inexperience 79

17 Telling the Truth 83

18 Symbols 88

19 The Mass Media 91

20 Tactics 96

21 Enemies 105

22 The Uses of Militancy 108

23 Sectarianism 112

24 Winning and Losing 116

25 A Call to Political Action 120

Political Action

A great deal of political activity is routine day-in, day-out work, best left to professionals. Other people don't have time for it, though they are often doing work very much like it in organizations whose character is not overtly political. But routine performances are adequate only to routine occasions. In moments of crisis, the professionals often can't cope; or, given new perceptions of injury and injustice, they seem to be coping badly. Then the democratic system offers a standing invitation to the rest of us to enlist in political life, an invitation to commitment and participation. More rarely, the question is not of enlistment but conscription: the routines suddenly collapse, and harsh choices are forced upon large numbers of men and women.

One of the reasons the choices are so harsh is that they involve people in activity and movement who were passive before. These are not incompetent people (not all or most of them, anyway), but they are often innocent of the complications of political life. They are unaware of the personal risks involved, unprepared for enmity and contention, unaccustomed to the sheer endlessness of artful talk and manipulative behavior. Nevertheless, they act. In clubs, campaigns, movements, they articulate their sense of *something wrong* and press for change. This little handbook is for them, because they are inexpert, as I am, and in order that the little we learn will not become a trade secret.

Every man has his own sense of crisis and outrage. So long as this is not shared or widely shared, most of us deal with it, suffer from it, repress and forget it, in private. The solitary prophet makes his own wilderness of inattention, mockery, and withdrawal by talking to people unwilling to listen. It is (sometimes) worth trying, but most of us learn to keep quiet. Political action is only possible when expressions of outrage and prophecies of disaster meet a lively response, at least within some circle of our own acquaintances. We try them out on our friends. The actual decision to enter the political arena will almost certainly be made by a small group, but it should only be made by a group whose members have what might be called intimations of growth. Where do such intimations come from? Hopefully, from conversations and encounters with other people, hints of commitment, plausible signs of interest. Would-be activists must have some sense of their future constituency; they must know that so many people

will support the strike, attend the mass meeting, join the
march, before they put themselves forward and call for action.

I want to caution against the intimations of pure theory, the
products of a very specialized form of conversation. Political
discourse carried on within the narrow circle of academies
and sects does not produce—not alone—signs sufficient to
justify political action. Later on, I will take up some of the
problems of sectarian politics, but one feature of such politics
should be mentioned here: the willingness to act, in
disregard of present experience, on the basis of one or another
theoretical view of the future. Then parties and movements
are developed that are grounded on nothing more than the
tense expectancy of the faithful, and barring the occurrence
of the expected events, and given the likely occurrence of
unexpected events, the band of the faithful generally remains
small. There are ways of dealing with this difficulty, as the
long history of Christianity suggests, but there are many more
ways of not dealing with it. Hence the political sects of the Left,
each one the product of an initiative for which, whatever the
verdict of the future, the present was not ripe.

But sectarian initiatives are at least preceded by extended
speculations about consequences and outcomes. Much more
dangerous is the recklessness suggested by the maxim of a
Jacobin leader in 1793: *"On s'engage et puis, on voit."*
I commit myself, and then . . . I see what happens. That is,
whether or not I have support, whether or not my commitment
is retrievable, whether or not other people are affected, and, if
so, how they are affected, I act in the hope of unpredictable

goods and even, perhaps, without any hope at all. What this most often means is that my action derives from personal rage and frustration so intense, so unbearable that doing something now seems far more urgent than producing effects later on. I have, in fact, had such feelings, and I have seen other people possessed by them. But political motivation is something quite different. We become political men when we act for public and not private reasons, or at least for public in addition to private reasons, and when we imagine our effects in terms of other people as well as ourselves. Political action is action with or for others, and while we may think our personal feelings very important (as we all do), they are, in fact, less important than the inevitably impersonal feelings for other people that are involved in acting with this group, for this group, against that group of men and women whom we cannot really know.

Large numbers of men and women ready to act together without knowing one another, and in disregard of the professional and his routines—these are the makings of the political moment. The makers of the moment are some smaller number of men and women who recognize the readiness and give it public expression. The readiness itself has two sources. Common injury, class interest, ethnic solidarity produce a kind of citizen politics most likely to evolve into professionalism, most likely to leave behind permanent defensive alliances and associations. Only the beginning moments of the labor movement (and then of each new union), for instance, provide clear examples of amateur activism—though every strike turns up new activists free of professional sophistication yet politically competent in surprising ways. On the other hand, the struggle for women's suffrage remained throughout a citizens' movement and never produced a professionally run feminist union, in part because no ongoing organization of women was (or was thought to be) necessary once suffrage was won.

Moral outrage, anger, and sorrow for injustices done within our own society, or by our government overseas, produce a kind of citizen politics most likely to remain the province of citizens, largely because its incidence and endurance are so unpredictable. Professional politicians seek out, sometimes, the support of such citizens, but they are not likely to join them. In any case, the politicians are rarely there at the beginning. The first attempts to cope with the crisis, to end the injustice, begin without them, and despite them, when a group of citizens holds a meeting, argues about strategies, and plans a new organization.

Beginnings

The first task is to find the support one believes is there, to reach out somehow to unknown but sympathetic people. In order to do that, the little group of activists must appear to be more than it yet is. Beginnings are rarely straightforward; they trade on unpredictable futures. It is necessary at once that there be a name, a speculation on the movement to follow, but worth thinking about, since names are not easy to change. After the name, an address, a letterhead, a list of sponsors, a statement and a program, a press release. All this may seem embarrassing and pretentious to the men and women who put it together; they can still meet, and probably will, in each other's living rooms. But there is no other way. They must make themselves visible, and it is not enough simply to stand up.

Political movements are begun by throwing together a façade, behind which activists rush about trying to raise a building. Often enough, they fail; the façade collapses before there is any shelter behind it. But if they have chosen their moment wisely, the first little group will find people to help it along. Other groups will spring up on the same model and will want to affiliate with the first, not necessarily because it is larger or more powerful, but simply because it is first. The initiative belongs to its members, as do, for a time at least, the crucial decisions.

Sometimes the original group is already a political association —a sect or party—and its members are political professionals, though most likely of a marginal sort. Then the façade they put up is especially important. They must look like ordinary citizens if they are to attract significant support. This sort of disguise should probably be encouraged; in many cases it is the functional equivalent of good intentions. And, assuming a worthwhile cause and an attractive façade, even knowl-edgeable activists may do well to join, for the sake of the others, so to speak; and, if necessary, to make trouble later on.

With regard to many issues, national committees of one sort or another already exist, founded, sometimes, long ago, and sustained with more loyalty than wisdom. Nevertheless, it is often sensible to try to begin under the banner of an established organization and to work with or (in time) take over its national office. Otherwise, energy will be wasted differentiating oneself from the existing group and fighting with its staff. There is often real help to be had, and the status of a local branch is nothing to be ashamed of. But if the existing group has come to be identified with defeat, or with some idiosyncratic and isolated leader, or with sectarian styles of political action, then not only a fresh start but also the appearance of a fresh start is vitally necessary. Citizen activists gain a great deal, in such cases, if their movement looks shiny and new.

Quiet men and women often exaggerate the importance of their own outrage, their long delayed decision to *do something*. If they are moved, how can the rest of the world stand still? But it is always best to plan one's moves on the supposition that most of the world will stand still, that established institutions and social practices will survive the shock. All that has changed is that some group of people has decided to use the pronoun "we," and to act together. Nor is it the case in a democratic society that this decision challenges the political system. Quiet citizens are the resources of a democracy, saved up, we are told, for those moments when professionalism fails. They may feel unconventional; they may behave unconventionally; but their intermittent forays into the political arena are by now one of the conventions of democratic politics. That doesn't mean that what they do isn't important, nor that it isn't sometimes dangerous. Using democratic rights puts them at risk: now there are men and women—now there are enemies —threatened by that use. For this reason above all, it is important for activists to know what they can and cannot do, and never to indulge themselves (or frighten their enemies) with fantasies of social and political changes they cannot actually bring about.

Revolution is such a fantasy, less common than is often thought, but worth dealing with early on. Citizen activists may aim at this or that fundamental change, but they cannot hope to make a revolution. It is not very often that anyone actually *makes* a revolution. Revolutions happen, and all sorts of people find themselves, unexpectedly, participants in the happening. Ordinary citizens will be among them (often yearning not to be), but at such moments it is the professionals, newly recruited professionals perhaps, who take charge. Power of the ultimate sort is at stake, and no one contends for such power in a part-time way, or carries on simultaneously a nonpolitical career, or retires casually from the struggle once some point of special interest has been won. But these are the characteristics of citizen activists; simply listing them helps explain why amateur politics is most often parasitic on the routines of a more or less stable democratic system. The crises and outrages that set off the political activity of ordinary citizens are serious enough, but they occur within a system that is not yet in a state of total crisis and that protects even the irregular responses of its members. Most men and women join the movement counting on that protection. It isn't absolute, as they will learn, but it is a great deal more than revolutionaries have any right to expect.

Giving the system a "last chance" is another fantasy. This suggests that revolution is the next step if citizen activism in general, or this particular citizens' campaign, fails to carry the cause to victory. But activists have no business imagining that they will win right away; they are a minority, probably a small minority, of the country. They must risk failure, and they ought to be aware that the most likely consequence of failure is not revolution at all, but the fragmentation of their movement and the retreat of many citizens from politics. Small bands of sectarian militants may then experiment with disruption and violence, fantastically imitating Jacobins and Bolsheviks. But this is rarely a serious business. One day, hopefully, there will be a new mobilization of activists, a reorganized movement, and another citizens' campaign—that is, another "last chance" for the system. *There is nothing else to do but try again.*

The real choice faced by the men and women who plan these successive attempts is between two kinds of politics, both of which have conventional names, though they can each be pursued in a variety of irregular ways. The two kinds are pressure politics and electoral politics, and I am inclined to think that there are no other kinds. To choose pressure politics means to try to influence those people who already hold power, who sit in official seats, who may even be responsible for the outrages against which the movement is aimed. To choose electoral politics is to try to dislodge those people and plant others in their seats, not necessarily or even probably the leaders of the movement, more likely whatever alternative set of professional politicians the system provides. Of course, the two choices overlap in important ways; they are often pursued simultaneously, with stress being put on the first only until some group of professionals adopts the cause. But it is worth emphasizing the two simply because they exhaust the range: changing the policies men make and changing the men who make policies. Changing the political system within which policy is made is rarely a real option for citizen activists.

It is never easy to know when to shift from pressure to electoral politics, whether at any given moment (and the moments are recurrent) to enter or to avoid the campaign of this or that candidate or party. On the one hand, electioneering is the sort of politics citizen activists are most familiar with, know best, probably do best. On the other hand, they often feel that their break with the routines of the system precludes it. They have come to distrust the promises of professional politicians. They are in search precisely of a politics that does not require them to support candidates who are only barely better than their opponents and who have, most likely, weak and vacillating positions on what the activists believe is the crucial issue. Sentiment of this sort is entirely justified. It is, after all, what makes the movement possible in the first place.

But assuming that pressure politics (petitions, mass meetings, marches, and so on) doesn't lead to a change in government

policy, electoral politics is a necessary next step. The
movement can't avoid it, even if supporting conventional
candidates and parties involves some compromise of its
principles. It is only a question of when, and to that there is
no specific answer. The general answer is: not until the
movement is strong enough to force fairly clear positions upon
the professionals and to exercise some control over them
once they have won.

This general rule sometimes suggests to activists that they
must run their own candidates or that they must join in a new
political party. A single-issue educational campaign, even
with victory inconceivable, may be a useful activity; whether
it is or isn't in any particular case is a tactical decision. A new
party is something quite different. It involves the movement in
a coalition with many other groups and so defines its position
on many other issues; it requires a commitment to an elaborate
program and to broad social change. That is a commitment
many of the activists would probably like to make, but it is not
what first brought them together, and it is not what holds them
together with other activists in the movement. Nor is it at all
clear that a new party and a struggle for social change on a
wide front is the best (the easiest or the quickest) way to carry
their own cause to victory. There are, in fact, two very different
strategies entangled here, which will have to be separated out
in the course of movement debate and action. Two questions
are crucial: Should the citizens' movement be committed to
single-issue or to multi-issue politics? Should the movement
be organized as a single constituency or a coalition?

Defining the Issues

4

New political movements generally take shape around a single issue—a wrong being done to the people who join or to some other group with whom they have political connections or moral sympathies. The activists are likely to disagree about much else, but this sense of injury or indignation they must share. As they work together, they may come to share more than this. Issues related to the original one come into view, and the values that underlay their first choice of action may lead them to choose again, to extend the range of their movement. Sometimes, however, and probably more often, new issues have opposite effects: the movement splinters; its members discover that they are really radically different from one another.

These different possibilities lead from the first to very different views of what the movement should be like. Some members insist that its focus should be resolutely fixed on the single issue that brought them together. Necessarily they attribute great importance to that issue: they believe or they say that the world will be different (and much better) once it is resolved. They blind themselves, sometimes willfully, to the entanglements of social and political life, to all the obstacles that lie between the particular victory they may in fact win and the transformations they hope for. They choose the part over the whole; that is, they have or choose to have perceptions of the part, but only visions of the whole. Other members seem to be more realistic. They try to fit the single issue into a complex of problems. They try to develop a coherent program for social or political change. Then they want the movement to adopt their program, to switch from single-issue to multi-issue politics. Perhaps that means that some activists will drop out, but ultimately, they say, the movement will be stronger and, because of its wider scope, will appeal to more, not fewer, people. The tendency of this second group is to turn the movement into a political party.

Now, it is a great deal harder to launch a party than a movement, as American history amply demonstrates. Or, to make the same point in another way, it is all too easy to establish a very small political party, an association of activists who have the same position on almost everything. But a party that grows, losing something of its coherence yet retaining a common program—this is an extremely rare and difficult achievement. It may well be the "right" response even to very particular wrongs, rooted in sociological sophistication, reaching toward intellectual complexity and completion. But it requires too much from too many people—too much time, energy, money, above all too much commitment—to be politically viable. The movement, with all its necessary pretension, is more nearly possible. And victories can be won through single-issue campaigns. Indeed, it is hard to think of any other kind of victory that citizen activists have ever won. Winning turns out, of course, to be something less than they expected. The end of child labor, the achievement of women's suffrage, prohibition and its death, the end of this or that war: none of these planted the new Jerusalem. Nor, however, were they or will they be without significant effects, for good or ill.

Issues should be defined so that victories can be won. This doesn't mean that one should be able to imagine winning tomorrow. The question is not so much of time as of particularity and limit. It is always possible to describe one social problem so that it involves every other, so that its solution requires the solution of every other problem and the transformation of society as a whole. This is one of the major achievements of Marxist ideology. But it is also possible to describe one social problem as if it stands alone or sufficiently apart from other problems so that it can be solved without doing anything else or waiting for anything else to happen. Neither description is true, though it is possible that the first is more sophisticated.

Political activity anywhere in a society obviously produces

adjustments, not necessarily transformations, everywhere. But the character and extent of these are almost impossible to predict. We make guesses and are usually wrong. In any case, action cannot and does not depend upon a true theory of social change. It requires a useful theory, or something less than a theory—a point of view, a set of opinions, an argument —that at least does not contradict whatever little we know to be true. And the most useful argument is one that imposes upon activists only one choice and only one fight at a time. They can always make further choices, join further fights, later on. Some members of the movement will want to plan ahead and should certainly do so, though not at the expense of the movement's immediate focus. That focus should almost certainly be on a single issue, an important issue, but simply stated: the vote, the war, the bomb. Activists and their spokesmen can safely exaggerate both the importance and the simplicity. Let victory bring its complications and disappointments.

Searching for
a Constituency

5

A constituency is a social base, a sector of society (ethnic group, age group, economic class, or whatever) within which the movement finds sympathy and support, from which it recruits members, for which it claims to speak. But this constituency is not given, like that of a congressman or senator. It presumably has objective characteristics; it recognizably exists in the sense that men and women sharing those characteristics exist. But it is not organized; its members may not be conscious of the identity they share; nor does it act as a single body. Activists can try to turn it into a single body, a self-conscious whole, a collective force; or they can try to build such a body from among its members. Often they do the second, while pretending to do the first.

•

Finding a constituency is not always a problem. The constituency of the labor movement is the working class; organizers know exactly where to look for support (though they may look elsewhere as well). Generally, movements seeking to respond to injuries or injustices endured by particular groups of people plausibly direct themselves to those same groups. But sometimes such groups are thought to be incapable of defending themselves; someone must act on their behalf. And sometimes a movement is aimed at a policy thought to be unjust or immoral, but which is not injurious, or not obviously injurious, to any group of possible political actors (a foreign war, for example). In either of these last two cases, constituencies may be particularly hard to search out and put together. Yet the historical evidence is clear: the available people in such cases are largely middle class, and they come from fairly distinct sectors of the middle class: urban professional families, suburban housewives, students, and so on. I am not concerned here with efforts to explain the peculiar capacities of the middle class for moral indignation, nor with the level of education, leisure time, child-rearing practices, or ethnic history of its members. What is more important for our purposes are the special difficulties that middle-class activists have in dealing with their own people, their inevitable constituency.

The choice of action requires a break with the conventional world. Usually this is a break with the middle-class world, and the men and women who make it are eager to differentiate themselves from the people they have left behind.

Differentiation takes a great variety of forms, and many of these are harmless enough: small badges, self-awarded, for distinctive conduct. One form, however, is not harmless at all: the adoption of an ideology that focuses the new activist's hostility on his own past, his social or ethnic origins, his former friends and neighbors. This is appropriate for a revolutionary, perhaps, but it makes citizen activism a great deal harder than it need be. Activists do best if they begin by assuming that there are more people like them where they came from. They are wrong to think of themselves as unusual people, though they may well take pride in their resolution and energy. If they are in fact different in more fundamental ways, they are unlikely to be able to act effectively. *Begin where you are*—this is one of the central maxims of moral life, but in the life of a political movement it is often necessary to begin where you were.

This is especially important in the case of student activists. Their first constituency is the campus; their second is the world of their parents. They prefer often enough to go almost anywhere else (though they are unlikely to end up anywhere else). But there can be no doubt that they are most effective among the people they literally left behind, who are glad (mostly) to see them back. And they ought, whatever their preferences, to be as effective as they can.

I don't want to deny the need to reach or try to reach beyond immediately available constituencies. The efforts of middle-class activists to organize "in the community"—which usually means among working-class men and women—are sometimes worthwhile. For sometimes there are plausible signs that a working-class base can in fact be won or some substantial number of people recruited to the work of building their own base. But this is a foolish effort if there are no such signs, if the sole reason for not organizing elsewhere is the ideologically rooted belief that members of the middle class are different from "the people." In fact, of course, like everyone else, they are the salt of the earth.

It's necessary to think twice before turning the movement loose on "the people." Efforts to reach beyond the middle class are so often ruined by the arrogance or condescension of the citizen activists involved. Their good intentions are transparent, but so, unhappily, is the assurance of superior wisdom that is the badge of their class. The truth is that the class barrier is painfully difficult to break through, and the difficulty is not reduced simply because activists agree on the importance of making the breach. This is not a boundary that one can just dash across. Indeed, the more sudden and seemingly uncalled for is the attempt, the more certain it is to fail. Failure can be seen clearly, I think, in the way workers look at students leafleting at a factory gate: "Who are you?" they seem to be saying. "Why are you here *today*? Where will

you be *tomorrow?*" The effect is not much better when
students spend a summer inside the factory. On the other
side of the class line, a man is a stranger for a lot longer than
two months. He is betrayed every time he opens his mouth,
even if his rhetoric is as radical as it can be.

It makes more sense first to approach the leaders of whatever
organizations are established among the people one is trying
to reach: unions, churches, veterans' groups, community
clubs. Many citizen activists explicitly assume that these
leaders are not to be trusted. They are where they are,
however, because people trust them, and unless some
support can be found in their ranks, no other success can be
expected. The notion, so common on the left, that workers
must be organized "from below" is one of the clearest
examples of the arrogance of the organizers: they assume
they have some message to deliver that has never yet been
thought of, let alone argued and championed, by leaders and
would-be leaders within the working-class community itself.
They are almost certainly wrong, as a more humble approach
might well demonstrate.

Once contacts have been made, it is possible to think either
of organizing a local branch or forming an alliance of some
sort with groups that already exist. In either case, the actual
work must be done by people established in the community.
No serious political enterprise can be sustained for long by
outsiders—though it is always possible to make a few converts
and pretend to be leading a mass struggle. If local activists
don't take charge, it's best to give up and begin again

somewhere else. If they do take charge, they must be given their head. In time, the cause will be described in new accents; activity will take on a new style. It's all to the good if the movement comes to look very different in different parts of the country or even of the city.

When working among the poor, there is one thing that must never be forgotten: they have more immediate and pressing concerns than those of the movement. The worst kind of middle-class bias is the assumption that everyone else has, or ought to have, leisure, disinterest, and a passion for distant goods. In fact, for many people, a cause, even their own cause, is a luxury they can only occasionally afford. So a conventional politician who provides routine and necessary services easily wins a larger following than citizen activists with a program for Utopia, and he probably deserves the following he wins. His followers are rational men, not the victims (not, at least, in any simple sense) of oppression or "false consciousness." That is a reason, of course, for the movement staff to provide whatever services it can: day care, legal help, advice on available welfare programs. It is also a reason for seeking out conventional politicians and urging local activists to run for office. Among the poor, the movement cannot live on the cause alone; that is not, or not necessarily, a reason for giving up its single issue, but it does mean that it must ally itself with political groups and ambitious individuals who address themselves to other issues as well.

Coalitions

When political activists are successful, even minimally
successful, they not only add members to their own
organizations; they also bring other organizations into action.
The people they find are not facsimiles of themselves: they
have, or many of them have, different interests and loyalties,
different notions about appropriate channels. If they are
to become active, they will probably do so only within their
own groups. Some of these are established groups, their
leaders suspicious of the movement, sensitive about their own
prestige; some are as new as the movement itself, their
members equally hopeful, but with some scheme or plan all
their own. Some of them have only a peripheral interest
in the cause; some are ready to take it on, full time, at least for
a while. In any case, the movement must now consider the

relative advantages of the many different kinds of cooperation, alliance, and coalition.

With all the good will in the world, cooperation is not easy, and in practice one must make do with considerably less good will than that. The crucial problem is that the different organizations compete with one another. They find themselves fighting for a limited supply of members, money, media coverage, and so on. To some extent, the single-issue movement can reduce the intensity of these fights and save itself a lot of trouble if it sticks to its own issue, promising, in effect, to go away once the cause has been won. Then it is less of a threat to ongoing groups, such as labor unions and political parties, whose leaders can now hope, if they cooperate, to inherit some of the people mobilized by the movement. But there is bound to be conflict, perhaps especially among groups with more or less similar or overlapping goals. They will disagree about strategies, aim at different constituencies (but compete in practice for the same core of activists), accuse one another of stupidity, fearfulness, and even betrayal.

For all this, alliances and coalitions are possible and necessary. The familiar maxim about strange bedfellows is, in fact, an injunction: it is the aim of political action, of day-to-day argument and maneuver, to get people into the same bed who never imagined they could take a peaceful walk together. But there are political (and moral) guidelines to be followed in establishing these peculiar intimacies, and citizen activists don't always succeed in plotting the appropriate

course between puritanical fastidiousness and eager
promiscuity. It is mostly a question of time and place, but also,
as in moral life generally, of character. Some groups put
themselves beyond the pale; sometimes it is necessary to
say that with this or that organization, whose official policy
requires, say, a defense of Nazi or Stalinist terror, no alliance
of any sort is possible. This announcement is itself a political
act, which lets people know something they have a right to
know about the character of the movement. But when the
questions at issue are of lesser moment, citizen activists ought
never to make public display of their virtue. With ordinary
corruption and opportunism, as with disagreeable opinions,
they can deal—and they had better deal with them. The
only question is on what terms.

The movement is best able to handle temporary alliances,
planned with specific ends in view. Movement leaders should
take the initiative in proposing particular actions, for which
they can solicit particular kinds of help. They must expect, of
course, to pay some price for the help they get and should
always calculate in advance the various prices they are
willing to pay for the gains they hope to make. Cooperating
organizations will probably want to contact their own
members, distribute their own literature, have a speaker on
the platform, and so on. This is fine if, in return, they can turn
out so many people, provide so many marshals, raise so much
money; but it is a serious mistake if the "so many" and the
"so much" are too little. Even with groups that can really
help, negotiations are bound to be tricky. The movement is
torn between the desire for unity and success and the

(legitimate) fear of being misrepresented or even
overwhelmed in a welter of dissident groups and programs,
sectarian slogans, and irrelevant speeches. Obviously,
decisions here must vary with cases, but it is worth warning
against one very common form of blackmail.

Movement leaders are often afraid to break with groups to
their left—even if small, undisciplined, and of little
likely help—and so they are sometimes dragged into actions
considerably more militant than those they had planned. The
fear is not entirely senseless: far-left militants look more
committed, ready to work longer hours and take greater risks;
they evoke a naive kind of awe from many new activists. To say
no to them appears either cowardly or half-hearted. Yet it is
often necessary to say no—for three reasons which may
serve as guidelines for coalition-making in general: to
preserve the identity of the movement; to keep open the
possibility of future alliances with the largest available groups;
and to continue to attract citizens presently uncommitted or
advancing cautiously toward new political positions.

The important business of building long-term coalitions is
probably best left to political professionals. It requires some
delicacy and an almost endless capacity for compromise, and
neither of these is (or ought to be) a strong point of citizen
activists. Ongoing cooperation is only possible if the various
movements with their different constituencies can be drawn
into an organization that is greater than any of them and
promises gains to all of them. The appropriate organization is
the mass party, whether newly formed or old and established.

The promises are recognizably those of men seeking office. Citizen activists should aim at mobilizing their constituency so that this or that party will want to incorporate it and this or that office-seeker will want to make promises to it. Activists win most often by forcing their single issue into the platform of a major party, and then delivering their constituency at the polls. But they also lose, sometimes, by getting absorbed in party politics before they have mobilized a constituency of their own. Professional politicians prefer to bargain in the vaguest possible way with the largest possible groups. Movement activists must hold off until they can demand terms as specific as possible.

Young activists can occasionally choose the communities where they want to work, but most citizens simply are where they are. And to some degree, at least, the problems they face and the choices they have to make depend on just where that is. Citizen politics is most interesting, most difficult, and often most bizarre in the great metropolitan centers and the university towns. Here activists need never fear that they will find themselves alone—not for five minutes at a time. Their numbers are sufficiently large to make for self-sustaining activity. They are less dependent on national offices, programs, and publicity than are their counterparts in small towns and suburbs. Much of their sustained activity, however, is factional feuding and sectarian intrigue. They are absorbed in one another. Occasionally it is possible—and it always

looks possible, which is what makes politics so interesting—
to mobilize large numbers of people in a single movement for
a cause. This happens most readily in the context of a
national campaign: only then are the stakes high enough to
pull activists out of the local wars, or to pull new people in.

Politics is more serene in small towns and suburbs, where
many of the problems I shall be discussing hardly arise. Often
a fairly small group of people—the same group—enlist in
every political movement. Wearing different hats, they defend
different causes, and they rarely find themselves competing
with anyone else. Coalition politics is easy in such a setting.
But it may be a problem just to keep going and an even
greater problem to persuade new people to join so visible and
isolated a group. Here a sense of identification with an outside
movement is absolutely crucial, and a national office can
provide valuable services, making it possible for the local
group to carry on a variety of activities month after month,
year after year. The national office is itself sustained by such
local groups, which somehow survive without ever expecting
to. Militants from the metropolitan areas tend to be
contemptuous of these local "do-gooders," but that is always
a mistake. The "do-gooders" do good: they give the
movement a presence and a base in times and places where
the militants can't hope to supply either.

Whenever a nationwide campaign gains momentum, however,
many of these groups will be overwhelmed, inundated by new
members, unable to cope with the sudden end of a familiar
and peaceful isolation. Some of the people they trained

will hang on to provide continuity and leadership for whatever new organizations spring up. But power at such moments flows to the center (and out again in the form of itinerant organizers and campaign workers), or to the great cities where there are important victories to be won. If the campaign fails, the local groups will pick up the pieces and carry on.

The interconnections between local and national politics in the United States are extraordinarily complex. Though governmental decision-making is increasingly centralized and the media make it more and more difficult to sustain local activities that have no national significance, political power continues to be diffused, unevenly spread throughout the fifty states. This is especially so in political off-years—three out of every four in electoral politics and more than that, probably, in the politics of most movements. People are trained for political action, loyalty is accumulated, organizations are slowly built up, all at the local level.

It is inevitable, therefore, that movements test the devotion and commitment of would-be leaders by their willingness to work at this level, to organize and agitate in relative obscurity, in small communities or urban neighborhoods. But it would be wrong to count too much on what activists commonly call "base-building," virtuous as it is, for there are fairly narrow limits to what can be accomplished without the spur and spectacle of life on the summit. Most causes must finally be won in Washington or on the way there. Whenever possible, then, the movement must project the image of a national struggle, even if nothing is happening except in San Francisco and New York. But its members must not be taken in by their own projections. The movement is a mirage unless it has, and at crucial moments can demonstrate that it has, a substantial following dug in here and here and here across the country. The national image sustains local activity, but only local activity can make the image real.

Three Organizational Structures

The political organizations of citizen politics can be divided roughly into three sorts, according to the location of power within them. It is possible to make moral claims about the superiority of one or another of the three, and such claims form a large part of movement debate. But I am inclined to think that each has its appropriate time and place. To argue about how *this* decision should be made makes sense and is often necessary. To argue about decision-making in general usually doesn't make sense and isn't necessary.

The most common organizational structure is that of the *front group.* Here power is firmly held by a central staff or by the group of men (sometimes a party or sect) that puts the staff together and pays its members. The wider membership has no power at all and rarely any active role to play. It is made up of people who allow themselves to be used. They lend their names and money, and sometimes their physical presence, to a cause. They presumably approve the cause, though they are sometimes deceived or deluded about its precise character. Or they trust some set of sponsors who have previously approved the cause, but who accept no responsibility for its day-to-day working out. Nor do the members (or more loosely, contributors, petition signers, demonstrators, and so forth) accept responsibility. They are not committed to any ongoing activity or involved in the internal politics of the organization. In the front group all politics is staff work.

The front group is correctly called an elitist structure. It tends steadily toward professional routine as staff members learn that from this sort of work they can make a living (more often, a living of sorts). It opens the way to manipulation and deceit whenever the staff decides that it can acquire a sufficiently large and impressive front only by disguising the nature of its activities. Nevertheless, citizens are not wrong to lend their names, make their contributions, attend rallies and demonstrations—sometimes—at the behest of this or that elite group. For there are important political victories most readily won by a competent staff that is relatively free to maneuver and at the same time to demonstrate mass support. I should add that such a staff is never entirely free; it is bound to the cause by the implicit threat of mass desertion.

Pressure politics is often organized on the model of the front

group: the massive civil rights and anti-war demonstrations of
the 1960's were essentially staff operations. In such cases,
members of the central staff represent the interests or values
of the participants to the rest of the world. They petition
public officials, lobby in Congress, appeal to the country
through the mass media, plan and publicize the march or
rally itself. But the staff activists are by no means elected
representatives. They begin, more likely, with interests and
values of their own, then search out and put together the
constituency for which they speak. The front group is ideal
for the focusing and magnification of opinion. It is able to
generate large-scale support, or the appearance of
large-scale support, for this or that political position, precisely
because such support does not require time-consuming or
difficult work.

The work is done by the staff, which may also provide
specialized services not otherwise available; thus the legal
defense committee, publicizing some outrage of the judicial
system in order to raise money for an appeal or to lobby for
political intervention—while at the same time, perhaps,
building sympathy for the politics of the defendants. The
last of these is the least serious: the sympathy won is suitable
only for instant display; it is unlikely to be deep-rooted or
long-lasting. Staff work does not go very far in creating
political consciousness, even when its other victories are
impressive.

This is especially clear in election campaigns, which are

run most often on the front-group model. The candidate is not
chosen by the men and women who come to his aid; nor are
strategic or even tactical decisions made by the volunteer
workers. They do not determine (though they may affect) the
candidate's position; they do not always know what that
position is, or how serious or firm it is. They trust the
candidate, and the work they do for him tends to intensify,
even as it capitalizes on, that trust. Partly for this reason, it
does not always intensify their commitment to the issue or
program of the movement—unless they come into the
campaign as members of movement groups structured very
differently from the campaign organization itself.

The front group is not an instrument for sustained popular
mobilization. Its staff can collect large numbers of signatures
or even turn out thousands of people for an occasional
demonstration or an election canvass. But ongoing activity
requires a structure within which significant powers rest,
at least formally, with the mass of activists. The second model,
then, is *centralized democracy,* where the leadership is
directly or indirectly elected by the members and responsible
to them. Some degree of participation in internal politics by
the members is here presupposed. The strength of the
movement derives from the legitimacy that this participation
confers on the center. The center can issue commands that
are widely accepted; it can order a strike, demonstration, or
election campaign with the assurance that men and women
in large numbers will act together and do as they are told for as
long as necessary. That, at any rate, is the ideal: a democratic

movement can achieve an extraordinary discipline because it is founded on the consent of the disciplined (though also, sometimes, on class or ethnic solidarity).

It is rarely the case, however, that a large number of activists participate in the internal politics of the movement they support, and so the organization often assumes a dual character. The supporters are, in effect, a front, not, or not merely, for the central staff, but rather for a core of activists who rely on them for financial, moral, and occasionally physical support. Behind the front, there is cadre democracy, the self-government of the activists. This dual structure is one of the most useful for citizen politics, since it permits an easy movement between the wider following and the core. It is especially common among those local groups (in the anti-war movement, for example) that often provide the mass support necessary for national staff operations. Their cadres decide to participate, and call on their followers to participate, in demonstrations and elections they don't themselves plan or control. But they do plan and control their own participation and sustain a strong commitment to the cause. In such groups, both the demands that can be made on the followers and the freedom of the cadres are limited, but these limitations roughly fit the needs of citizen activism.

Centralized democracy without the dual structure is most suitable to parties, sects, and unions that need strong and stable leadership and sometimes make severe demands on their members. This is only possible if there is general agreement on policy and program. The democratic movement, in contrast to the democratic state, relies on a fairly tight consensus which most often takes the form of closely shared economic interests or a common ideology. Given this consensus, however, democratic controls on the leadership are often relaxed or even entirely surrendered, with results not very different from those that follow the same surrender in the state. Sects and unions are often formally democratic but in practice are run as autocracies. Then citizen activism is relevant only to the occasional rebellions that challenge the autocrats.

When no consensus at all exists, the best model for political activity is *federalism.* Here power rests with a number of centers, most often distributed geographically, each perhaps organized somewhat differently—as autocratic sects, cadre democracies, staff fronts, and so forth—all of them only loosely and informally coordinated. Every new proposal must be debated by each local. This project will be pressed by one, something quite different by another. Local option is the rule. The coordinating committee accumulates power only by convincing each local separately, and its power endures only for the length of whatever project is agreed upon. Federalism is a way of reflecting and coping with disagreements, but it has another feature often valued by citizen activists: it increases the number of people involved in decision-making; it decreases the possibilities of elitist manipulation (or, it multiplies and disperses the elite groups).

Unless there are significant victories to be won at the local level, federalism is the least effective pattern for political action. Local option deprives the national leadership of both authority and initiative; it virtually precludes negotiation or alliance with other political forces; it makes even short-term planning extremely difficult. It is probably best seen as an early stage in the development of citizen politics, when new groups are springing up and no "government" has yet emerged. But it often survives for a long time, even after many activists have despaired of its effectiveness, simply because no one can figure out how to wield together or overcome the local power centers.

If the original group of activists hopes to retain control of the growing movement, they obviously cannot choose a federal structure. They may simply maintain the façade they first raised and work out of an office behind it, or they may try to win mass support as a reward for their initiative. The last of these is the most interesting, since the activists will certainly encounter opposition. Conflict is inherent in a democratic organization. This is not necessarily divisive; it can have energizing effects, stimulating internal debate, generating a kind of competition in effectiveness. But it also raises, often in dramatic fashion, the question of leadership. For the best political organization may turn out to be not the one that is best organized but the one that is most ably run.

A surprisingly large number of people do not want political power. They have no eagerness for command, no thrusting willfulness. They want to do the right thing; they also want someone to tell them what the right thing is. So it is one of the major difficulties of a new movement that leaders cannot easily be recruited from among its rank and file. The individuals who do put themselves forward tend to have previous political experience and holdover commitments, personal or ideological, that are sometimes incompatible with the proclaimed aims of the movement. Would-be leaders may well discover in citizen activism not a movement for a cause but a vehicle for their own ambitions. Two sorts of people, above all, need to be considered here: disgruntled professionals and sectarian militants. Both sorts are or can be useful to the movement, but they are also predatory on the movement, and it is a mistake to allow either to displace whatever amateur leadership can be discovered or produced, however reluctant and inexperienced the amateurs are.

Politicians out of office are bound to see in any citizens' movement an opportunity for themselves. Some of them will commit themselves to the cause, with more or less fervor, and seek to absorb the activists into their own campaign organization. Within the movement, such commitments are often regarded with skepticism: why wasn't this or that professional politician committed before? (There is an obvious rejoinder: why weren't the citizens active before?) Perhaps the skepticism is justified, but the availability of opposition professionals is also an opportunity for the activists. Here is their crucial access point to the political system. What is necessary now is that the citizens find a way of providing the support the professionals need in their pursuit of office without ceasing to provide the stimulus and pressure they also need. In order to do this, the movement and the candidacy should probably remain distinct, even while members of the movement turn themselves into campaign cohorts for the candidate. There are two reasons for stressing this distinction. First, the candidate is unlikely to be willing to lead the movement as an independent force, either because he believes he must reach beyond its membership or, as in the case of Senator McCarthy in 1968, because his whole career and his sense of himself preclude movement politics. Second,

the movement must plan on surviving November, and it is not
always in the interests of the candidate that it do so. It's
necessary, then, to recognize the candidate as a national
(or local) leader while still supporting a separate movement
leadership.

Sectarian militants sense a different sort of opportunity in
the new movement: a chance to educate and recruit, to move
outside the narrow circles of their own routine activity. They
may also, of course, be committed quite straightforwardly to
the cause, but the cause, whatever it is, will have resonances
in their minds very different from those it has for other activists.
Insofar as the militants assume positions of leadership—as
they will do, for they are often extraordinarily diligent in
everyday politics—they will seek to fix the movement within
the structure of their own ideological program. In their hands,
citizen activism can be turned into a front for the sectarian
band or a channel through which committed individuals are
directed into the world of sect life. And then bewildered
citizens will flee the movement, retreating nervously before
the ideological intensity and the long-term planning of the
militants. In a very strict sense, sects are parasitic on
movements; ideological militants feed on indignant citizens.

But the militants can also provide important services to citizen
activists, and since the relation between the two can't be
avoided, just as the relation of professionals and amateurs
can't be avoided, it must be worked out so as to permit the
survival and growth of whatever political activity citizens

manage to launch. Professionals and militants seek to exploit
the movement; the movement must find ways to exploit them.
It must use the time, energy, competence, and zeal of the
militants for its own legitimate purposes without succumbing
to their ideology. On this or that project, they will work
feverishly, harder than anyone else, and certainly they should
be encouraged to do so. But they must also be denied what
they will surely regard as the just rewards of their toil. This
can only be done by an "indigenous" leadership confident of
its own purposes, freed from the delusions of instant victory
(which opens it to the professionals) and ultimate redemption
(which opens it to the sectarians). No great capacity for
organizational intrigue is necessary here. Leaders with a solid
base, in touch with their constituency, need only a little
resolution and ordinary stubbornness to win out.

Citizen activism has its own time scale, and its leaders must be
attuned to the implicit rhythms of less than total commitment,
part-time work, and (relatively) short-term goals. But here I
come back to the original difficulty: part-time and short-term
activists do not seek leadership positions, and tend not to
make self-confident leaders even when they are chosen by
their comrades. They must nevertheless be chosen and given
what support they need. I cannot think of anything more
important to the success of citizen politics (especially on the
local level) than the cultivation of citizen leaders. Capable
men and women are available. They appear in the midst of
every strike, demonstration, and election campaign. They
assume responsibilities, they cope with crises. They
disappear, however, as soon as the full-time politicians,

professional or sectarian, arrive on the scene and confidently start telling everybody what to do.

But those leaders know best what to do who know the people who have to do it. And that is why it is worth looking hard for ways to open political life to talented activists who have other lives to live. These same people must be encouraged to hang on when challenged and enabled to move out of their own local into the national office—and back again—when they are ready. One way to help them I will take up immediately: that is, to finance their activity so that they need neither commit themselves (and their families) to poverty nor seek out professional status and rewards.

Raising and Spending Money

The easiest way to get money is to ask for it. There are a variety of people to ask: wealthy and politically serious men and women who have to be convinced that this project and not that one deserves support; promoters and angels for whom politics is another kind of theater—they want only to be assured of fashionability and success; guilty nonparticipants who might like to march and demonstrate except for all the reasons they have for not doing so; and, finally, marchers and demonstrators themselves, some of whom, at least, can pay as they go. The first two groups must be approached in person; the others through the media and the mails. Activists don't often make good beggars, and here (elsewhere too) they should not hesitate to get professional help—and to pay for it.

But the best way to get money is to earn it (or some of it, since there is no way to avoid begging) through the conventional fund-raising activities of nonpolitical organizations. It is not puritanism, or not that alone, that leads me to insist upon the value of earning money. Fund-raising is an important activity because it enables large numbers of people to express their support for the movement in ways that also utilize their everyday competence and give them something important to do. Among the most demoralizing features of political life are the long spells of inaction, the time spent standing around or wasted in desultory debate and factional infighting. Fund-raising is both time-consuming and useful. Many people are accustomed to it and do it well; and the sense of a job to be done that can be done is a crucial factor in generating loyalty to the cause and self-confidence in the activists. So a successful auction, book fair, or bake sale is a (minor) triumph for peace, integration, women's rights, socialism, or whatever: so many people are doing something and not merely waiting for the Revolution. Political action has, I suppose its moments of glory, but activists must learn to serve proudly the gods of the commonplace.

The ways in which money is earned (and spent) affect also the constitutional balance of the movement. Internal democracy is fostered when money is earned by the members, even more so when it is initially accumulated by local branches. Members and locals are more likely then to insist on a say in spending it, and the center will be more sensitive to their opinions. (This is less likely when the members merely pay

dues to the center, especially if that payment has become
routine in one way or another.) Private contributors obviously
place power in the same hands they put the money in. They
help to build strong staffs or central committees. The causal
connection works the other way too: men who aspire to form a
strong central committee must search for financial backing.

However it is accumulated, the distribution of money is certain
to be a major focus of political controversy. Perhaps the most
crucial argument in new parties and movements, and one I
want to dwell on, is whether or not to pay campaign workers.
Freely given time and energy are an absolute prerequisite of
citizen politics; without that nothing is possible, and there is
great pressure to make do with that alone, or, at most, to pay
a bare subsistence to those activists who require it. After all,
how can one hire a man's enthusiasm? And how can he
charge the movement for doing what is (presumably) every
citizen's duty? Yet there are two problems with unpaid or
barely paid activists that must be faced if structure and
leadership are to be provided for any ongoing work. First,
payment is a crucial connection to the center. A man who
takes money is also likely to take orders. However much must
be said for the independent activist whose moral commitment
is his only connection to the movement, it remains true that his
cooperation and obedience cannot be guaranteed. It is never
certain that he is committed to these particular leaders or to
this particular program (rather than to the cause in general).
That is his strength, but sometimes the movement's weakness.
At certain key moments, in certain key positions, one simply
needs people who will do as they are told. Of course, there

are ties other than the moral bond and the cash nexus
(friendship is perhaps the most important in informal groups,
collective discipline in highly organized parties), but mostly
we take pledges and distribute money, and the possible
utility of the second should not be overlooked.

The second problem relates to the class and age of the
activists. Unpaid work comes most often from the young and
the well-to-do. The prototypical activist is the upper-class
student who often makes politics seem, like romantic love, a
matter of world enough and time. His devotion is profound,
his energy extraordinary, and, most important of all, his days
are free. Clearly, he will provide much of the manpower
necessary for any ongoing activity. But he cannot provide a
stable base for the movement; he is without roots in any
particular community. Adults must be brought in, not merely
as patrons and supporters but as workers. This requires that
work schedules be adjusted so as to permit part-time
participation. It also requires that some people be paid and
even that they be paid fairly well so that they can (temporarily)
give up their regular jobs and still support their families. The
movement must make its peace with a certain amount of
semi-professionalism since so many adults can't afford to be
amateurs in the literal sense. I should stress that they often
can't afford amateur status in other ways too. The movement's
readiness to pay them is a sign of the value it places on their
work, a sign they might not be willing to relinquish even
if they were financially able to do without the money.
Activists may disapprove of the need for such signs, but they
are not acting in the society they hope to create. They are

acting in this one and alongside its inhabitants with their peculiar needs. There is an alternative to all this, however, that should be discussed separately: the exploitation of the housewife, as common in the movement as in society at large.

Professional politics is overwhelmingly a man's world. In citizen politics, women play a much larger part. Indeed, they constitute a majority of the adult participants in many activities. Young activists, struggling to get something started "in the community," find women reachable in ways that men on the job are not (to them); and women with families and without jobs in fact have time to spare for politics—just as they have time to spare for the church, the PTA, hospital aid, and so on. Politics is not so different from these, though it is sometimes more important. So women are drawn in; they do important work and work at which they are often highly experienced. But they only rarely emerge as leaders, and they rarely make the weight of their experience and participation felt when crucial decisions are being made.

The reasons for this don't have much to do with citizen politics in particular. The subordination of women, especially older women, in the new party or movement is only one more example of their position in the old society. The conventional activities that women most readily take up in the movement are those that are most seriously underpaid out of it. And the part-time work that is easiest for women with children is everywhere undervalued, by no means peculiarly so in the movement. Yet in the movement as out of it, women defer to men—to young activists, political old hands, semi-professionals, and part-time leaders who meet, argue, bargain, and hand down decisions. Even when women play key managerial roles in citizen politics, they are usually excluded from the boards of directors and steering committees which assume ultimate responsibility for movement projects. Sometimes this exclusion has a political excuse; often, it has to be said, the women involved do not resist. Unsure of their political roles, nervous about their family commitments, lacking in self-confidence, they allow themselves to become the common laborers of the movement.

There are any number of objections to be made to this situation, and the most important I leave to the women themselves. I only want to point out one consequence of their subordination for citizen politics, that is, the ephemeral character of so many amateur movements. This is caused at least partly by the way in which power in these movements gravitates toward people who are marginal to any particular local community and away from people—a very large number of them women—who have established themselves where they are and assumed local responsibilities.

It is important to point out the contrast here with established political parties and labor unions which are essentially associations of adult males, rooted in their communities, supplemented and sometimes strengthened by Ladies Auxiliaries. Citizen politics can rarely take that form, since so many men are committed elsewhere. More important, it shouldn't take that form since one of its characteristic claims is to mobilize people who have been previously passive, unheard within the system. Women are one of its key constituencies, and their degradation is its especial loss. The failure of women to assume leadership positions or to participate fully in decision-making often leaves the new party or movement rootless, the ideological tool and sometimes the plaything of marginal men.

A church basement with cinder-block walls and linoleum floor, rows of uncomfortable metal chairs, a hundred or so people of all ages: here is a political meeting. Perhaps the people are leaders or representatives of local groups, perhaps they are simply members. I assume that they are meeting to make policy decisions and that they have met before. Typically, they have met too often before, and this meeting goes on too long. Too many people speak; the chairman flounders; older participants start to leave, fleeing homeward; no clear decisions are reached; another meeting is called for next Tuesday.

The tendency of citizen politics is toward democracy of expression, an equalitarianism of the vocal chords, which is

wonderfully exhilarating—a week, a month ago, these were
silent men and women—until it becomes exhausting and
tedious. Often the political assemblies of citizen activists turn
into what early Protestants called ''experience meetings,''
where one participant after another testifies to his motives
for joining the movement. Almost everyone wants a chance,
has a story to tell that is or may be relevant to the issue at
hand. And then to the testimonies are added the ideological
explanations of three or four political old hands, fiercely
antagonistic to one another, demanding equal time. Somehow
pressing issues are not resolved, though much that is said
is interesting, educational, even exciting. And the following
Tuesday fewer people come, above all, fewer older people,
married people, mothers, men and women with full-time jobs.
Expressive democracy is perfectly compatible with autocratic
decision-making. In fact, autocrats have a vested interest
in meetings of this sort.

If significant decisions are to be reached at meetings, there
are a number of simple rules to follow. It may not be so simple
to follow them: the question of how decisions are best made
inevitably gets tangled up with the question of which decisions
are best to make. Nevertheless, I think it is almost always
better to try to get the best decision out of a relatively large
meeting than to exhaust and depress the people who come
to meetings and then make the decision alone or with a small
group of allies. Better the church basement than the living
room, as soon as there is a choice. But this requires, first,
that meetings be infrequent and, second, that they be
managed.

The chairman must be someone capable of taking charge: cutting off irrelevant speeches, pressing the central issues, insisting on a vote before people start for home. Since the infrequency of meetings is possible only if subgroups get together in the intervals, committees appointed by the chairman and factions self-assembled from among like-minded activists must arrive at each meeting with proposals to make and opinions to defend. The chairman should know what these proposals and opinions are and who is going to present them, so that he can call on speakers in some plausible order. If he isn't in touch before the meeting, he won't be in control at the meeting. The chairman should never be surprised—which is not to say that he should always be successful in getting what he wants.

Running a meeting is often confused with manipulating it. That's not a silly confusion. Manipulating a meeting means running it with some purpose in mind beyond merely running it well. Chairmen often have such purposes in mind. That's why it is important to insist that they stick to some set of rules. A rough version of parliamentary procedure is probably best, but virtually any rules will serve, so long as they set limits to what chairmen (and others) can do.

It is often argued by new activists that no such rules are necessary among friends and comrades, but the idea of the ruleless meeting is, I'm afraid, hopelessly misconceived. It rests on the belief that agreements can be reached through uncontrolled and unlimited discussion if only the "spirit" of the meeting is sufficiently warm. But it generally isn't sufficiently warm, and most people, in any case, won't sit through the endless talk. When meetings are not run according to rules, their manipulation becomes more, not less, important —and much harder to detect. Formally shapeless discussion provides an absolutely open field for the manipulative craft of a few people. The crucial feature of orderly procedures is that they identify such people as responsible agents: the chairman himself, the mover of this or that motion, and so on. Meetings can be manipulated from the back row, but run well (and honestly) only from the front.

There are eighteen ways of manipulating a meeting, and it is best if there are eighteen groups, no less, trying to be manipulative, struggling to make their proposals sound like what everybody (really) wants. Then none of them is likely to have things all its own way. One of the problems of citizen politics is that most new activists come to meetings not knowing what they want to accomplish before they leave. Then they are in the hands of the others—professionals, militants, faction-men, and committeemen—who know exactly what they want. This difficulty can only be resolved over time, by making meetings as accessible, and procedures as transparent, as possible.

Meetings should be spaced so that part-time activists don't feel that the costs of attendance are prohibitive. They should never last so long that people with families or jobs feel that they have to leave. The rules should be clear, relatively simple, widely known. A great deal of work should be done by subgroups meeting at the convenience of their members.

These are seemingly easy matters, but they often involve considerable resistance to the pressures of activists with time to spare. Here are dangerous men, who feel that the movement needs their fullest devotion (it may need that) and who express that devotion by insisting, eagerly, ruthlessly, stubbornly, on one interminable meeting after another.

The central purpose of meetings is to involve the largest possible number of people in decision-making. The front group, therefore, can dispense with meetings almost entirely. It requires only rallies, which serve quite different purposes: ideological development, moral catharsis, the quickening of enthusiasm and solidarity. A good meeting can serve these purposes too, but it must do two other things as well: distribute power and impose responsibility. Unless it does them both successfully, the movement belongs to its leaders or to its staff.

A movement office isn't all that different from any other office; there isn't much to say about it. But a certain amount of political power is necessarily lodged there, and it is worth worrying about its precise lodging place. The office staff will consist mostly of part-time people, moving in and out, doing routine work. They will not find it easy to exercise much influence; they may not even try to do so, unless they are prompted. A number of full-time people will make day-to-day decisions, following loosely or strictly the policy directives of the central leadership and the mass meeting—loosely if the leaders stay away, closely if they come around. A leader who can run a meeting but can't or doesn't bother to make his presence felt in the office is unlikely to lead very effectively. The danger here is that the office may be "seized" by people who don't have the confidence of the mass meeting, but who don't need it because the leadership, knowingly or not, fronts for them. This is especially likely in a movement of part-time activists and part-time leaders. Perhaps a front group is appropriate to whatever activity they are all engaged in, but it isn't always appropriate, and the leaders (on behalf of the members) should be able to control the office if they choose to.

Staff power is sometimes described as a special kind of democracy: the necessary product of the right that people have to control the work they do. But the staff works *for* the movement and is responsible to it. Its members go to meetings like everyone else, probably more regularly, and, given an atmosphere of trust and good will, their position and knowledge will make them more influential than less active members can possibly be. The only other reward they can ask for the extra work they do is to be paid for it.

One last point: the records kept in the office—mailing lists, financial reports, correspondence—are very important, necessary if political work is to be sustained for any length of time or renewed after some temporary setback. Someone should look after them, and activists should insist that they are in fact looked after by people they know and trust.

Personal Relations in the Movement

15

It is a mistake to join the movement in search of love. Intimacy is neither a necessary nor a common feature of political life. The heightened emotions of collective action are peculiarly impersonal: they bring the individual into touch with too many other people to bring him into close touch with anyone in particular. Not love, but *amour social,* camaraderie, solidarity, are the unifying passions of the movement. And they are only sometimes intense and vivid passions. Most often, the size of the movement, the range of activities carried on by its members, the ever-present disagreements about strategy and tactics, the competition for leadership, the need to keep things together—all these tend to preclude the expression of strong feelings for particular people. (Strong feelings for abstract ideas are more commonly expressed.) Political association is the art of keeping one's distance: too close is a danger and a distraction; too far is a loss of control and influence.

Personal ties do exist within the movement, and sometimes they produce a kind of subpolitics that stands in various degrees of tension with the general commitment of activists to their cause. I am thinking especially of the subpolitics of the coterie and the entourage. A coterie is a sect without an ideology, a band of friends more deeply involved with one another than with the movement itself, more trusting of one another than of anyone else. Its members can be a divisive force (without ever intending division) simply because they intensify and exacerbate everyone's personal sensibilities. Ideally, I suppose, activists should leave at home their native alertness to slurs and snubs and heighten instead their sensitivity to the nuances of political disagreement. In practice, the two are mixed, held in some sort of rough balance. The danger of the coterie is that it tips the balance away from public disputes toward private intrigue. This is especially dangerous if the leadership itself is a band of friends, for many activists are sure to resent their exclusion who would not do so if they thought they were being excluded for political rather than personal reasons. Intelligent leaders will associate themselves with people who are not their friends, even with people they do not like.

An entourage is a band of people who wait upon a leader (and generally keep him from associating with anyone who is not an active admirer). Members of the entourage are loyal to the

leader, not at all to one another. Now loyalty to a leader is
one of the most profound and tenacious of political emotions,
but it is relatively rare, perhaps refreshingly rare, in the world
of citizen politics where leaders have all too little standing
with their followers. Occasionally a man or woman who has
been in trouble with the authorities, stood trial, or endured
imprisonment will win a special kind of following. But that is
not very dependable, particularly if a number of persons have
stood trial and endured imprisonment.

The entourage appears most often when some individual who
is powerful in the outside world joins the movement, bringing
his admirers with him. This sort of thing can cause problems
not only because it ruptures the easy familiarity and
camaraderie of the movement, but also because it stands in
the way of a cool assessment of the actual possibilities of
power and personality in political life. These possibilities are
generally greater than citizen activists are willing to admit,
especially when confronted by a leader and his entourage.
Once again, it is a question of keeping one's distance. Great
Men have a part to play, but it is not a good idea to have their
favorites write the script.

If love is uncommon in political life, hatred is common enough,
and it takes getting used to. One of the hardest things for
new activists to learn is that politics involves them constantly
in antagonistic relations with other people. A few of them
turn out to enjoy such relations, but most do not. Yet the
movement can offer only modest support to members
experiencing for the first time the anger and hostility of

political opponents. Its leaders and publicists can explain how
it is that political disagreements are so deeply rooted, social
and economic interests so fundamentally opposed. Other
members can offer their understanding and solidarity. But too
much should not be expected. Ultimately one draws on
personal resources to cope with the hatred of another man or
woman. Solidarity is a political tie, subject to political strains.
It may not outlast the first serious argument over strategy
and tactics. The movement itself is an arena of conflict and
antagonism. Commitment and camaraderie most often mute
the everyday disagreements. But sometimes they fail, and
then the internal polemics and power struggles can be intense
and bitter—especially so, perhaps, for those members who
had dreamed of unity and devotion.

Quackery and Inexperience

16

It is just possible that there is a higher proportion of fools in the movement (any movement) than in the general population. Certainly that is the way things look to the conventional eye. Marginal politics attracts marginal people who are ill at ease, resentful, graceless, unhappy, or frightened in the everyday world. They experience the perversions of common sense, perhaps in a profound way; foolishness, so to speak, is thrust upon them. The movement liberates them, or leads them to think they are liberated, and so it becomes an arena within which their repressed discontents are acted out, their secret nostrums revealed, often in naive and extravagant ways. They are set free to dress, talk, live in unconventional styles that may or may not be the styles of the future, but which serve now as expressions of hostility toward the present. A kind of diffuse outrage plagues the movement, a surplus of pent-up emotional energy which is equally dangerous when it floats freely and when it fixes upon a single theory of the world's ills. There is no easy remedy for all this. A solid organization and a lot of hard work can go some way toward transforming into disciplined indignation the latent hysteria that most political systems only repress and exploit. But until that transformation occurs, activists must suffer fools, if not gladly, at least patiently. They are all in rebellion against what passes for commonsense politics, and it is not easy (so they will learn) to sustain that rebellion without sometimes appearing senseless.

Inexperience is somewhat less of a problem, for politics is less an acquired skill than the professionals pretend. I don't mean that there isn't a lot to learn; there is. And there are moments, too, when professional advice can be very helpful. But the professionals make disastrous mistakes, and they seem to make them randomly. New activists sometimes find themselves in that enviable position best described by saying: they can hardly do worse than has been done. Or, if worse is always possible, so is better. It happens often that the chances of political life favor the amateur: because he tries new tactics, takes greater risks, works feverishly hard, conveys a sharp sense of excitement and urgency, exploits the enormous and perennial appeal of innocence. The last of these is the most interesting. I suppose inexperience is the easiest kind of innocence; it has the attraction of the *gauche* rather than the pure. But there is method in the *gaucherie;* it is an important vehicle for the expression of moral feelings.

So long as the outrage of the activists is not hysterical or their appearance outlandish, the combination of *gaucherie* and righteousness makes a powerful political force. There is a strong popular presumption in favor of the inexperience of a moral man and also of the morality of an inexperienced man. This is the secret of the anti-political (anti-professional) campaign—one of the most successful kinds of politics.

The difficulties of inexperience are most apparent when new activists absorb their first setback, or when they first realize that much of the work they have to do is unexciting, not all that different from the routines of conventional politics. It's the settling into the movement that is hard—the first campaign is delightful—and it is made much harder if one's fellow activists are struggling to sustain the drama of their own earliest encounters. They can do this for a while at least, largely by the frenetic way they talk to one another and to outsiders. And then the movement takes on a tense and heated quality that does not prepare its members even for the relatively short-term politics of citizen activism.

New activists eagerly play parts in each other's fantasies and imagine themselves involved in important battles for the cause. The real battles come as a shock. The dull, continuous work, the necessary discipline, the minor setbacks and disappointments, the indifference or hostility of most of the world, the need to come back tomorrow and do again whatever was done today: these are the initiatory experiences of political life. Until a significant number of citizens have survived them, there is no real movement at all, but only an

inchoate band of discontented men and women ready for
an adventure that may or may not have much to do with the
cause they espouse.

The tactical mistakes of inexperienced activists are endless
and unimportant. At any rate, they don't distinguish citizen
politics from any other kind. One learns and recovers, or not.
The real failures of new activists tend to be gross; they are
failures of nerve and endurance, marked by sudden
defections, wild talk, personal indulgence, dangerous
adventures. Against all these the movement must struggle
almost as energetically as against whatever feature of the
old society it is opposing. But its leaders must never forget
that the people who act out these failures are their own people,
their only hope for success. They cannot dissolve the mass of
activists and find another.

Talking is the most common form of political activity. Often people join the new party or movement eager to "do something" and then are frustrated and confused to find themselves mostly talking—to one another. They have to talk to one another in order to decide what to do, and whatever they decide is certain to involve talking with other people. Despite the skepticism they come to express—*only* talk, *mere* words—all this does have effects, even significant effects. I don't think that anyone who has ever attended a meeting can doubt that people are indeed swayed by skillful speech. They are also swayed, though probably in smaller numbers, by skillful writing. It makes sense, then, to try to say something about skill with words, though I cannot offer a treatise on rhetoric. I want to focus instead on the problem of truthfulness

in political speech, a perennial issue and one especially
pressing in the movement, which is so often racked by debates
between honest zealots and idiot Machiavellians. Two
questions are crucial: How complex (or simple) should
political arguments be? How straightforward (or evasive)
should political speakers and writers be?

Once a man has taken a stand on a particular issue, he is
tempted to take a stand on every issue. One thing leads to
another; everything interconnects. He is pressed toward a
total ideological position; he yearns for intellectual coherence,
unity, completion. Now a total view of political life, if it is
radical and new, requires a fairly elaborate language, a
complex jargon with its own intellectual and idiomatic
conventions. But it can often be summed up and presented,
precisely because of its total character, with breathtaking
simplicity. It can be expressed politically, at meetings,
marches, and demonstrations, in those stark slogans whose
loud reiteration is a hallmark of sectarian militancy and a
hostile act against the unbelieving world. If the unbelievers
turn away, as they naturally do, this does not mean that they
don't have slogans of their own. Professional politicians fully
understand the value of reiteration, though they can afford to
be quieter than the militants. Their catchwords also reflect
total views, not necessarily views recently worked out or even
thought about, but similar in the range of issues they touch
upon to those of the most ambitious sectarian ideologist. And
these conventional ideologies, which don't require a new
jargon, but are routine and automatic in common speech, are

believed, or at any rate accepted, by vast numbers of people.

When citizen activists break with some conventional view, they generally do so, or think they do so, for simple reasons. But as they involve themselves in political argument, they discover that one convention fits (roughly) with another. They are committed to more rethinking and worrying than they had anticipated. This is what makes so many of them suddenly available to anyone with a new ideology: they are prey for the militants. But the position of new activists is unstable in a much more important way. A few reassuring words from some politician in power may bring them quickly back to the old conventions and routines. So it is vitally important that those activists capable of speaking and writing undertake to explain to the others their new position.

They have a lot of explaining to do. They need to offer reasons for their move into what is actually a kind of limbo. Not one reason, but lists of reasons, for they are likely to be speaking to people of very different sorts from very different backgrounds. They cannot speak either in systems or in slogans. I think there is an important sense in which citizen politics, by its very character, is opposed to total ideologies in both their routine and their radical manifestations. Its participants are drawn away from conventional politics but remain uncommitted as a group to any single alternative. Their unity is partial and probably temporary, and their spokesmen should not pretend that it is anything else. They have to make arguments without claiming that the arguments they make are linked together in some complex whole. As for their style, it is not so much intellectual brilliance or any sort of verbal legerdemain that is necessary as what used to be called plain speech: simple language, a quiet tone, an air of calm, a slow pace. All this is reassuring, and none of it, I should add, is incompatible with anger. The worst thing of all is hysteria, in some ways the most sincere response to political crisis, but the most disturbing and frightening to uncommitted onlookers.

The great advantage that activists have is that they speak the same language as other citizens. They should continue to do so, elaborating the conventional catchwords in new ways, for example, rather than initiating one another into strange ideological idioms. They should challenge one convention at a time, as it becomes necessary, and in any given period as few as possible. Above all, they should establish priorities and stick to them: if the movement hopes to persuade people to oppose the war, for example, its members should not make radical pronouncements about sex or drugs or any other fashionable and exciting issue that catches their eye.

But this course of action may well seem less than honest to many citizen activists and, what is more important, to some of the most articulate among them. They have begun, perhaps, to rethink all their political beliefs; they see or think they see that this particular action has consequences throughout the political system; it must or it should lead to further action. They sense a more general crisis, once they have cut their ties and begun to act, than they ever did before. They are tempted by one or another radical ideology. And they want to tell all, to describe with the utmost sincerity their own evolving position. They should do this if they like within the movement, certainly among the core of activists, even though most of their speculations about the future, like everyone else's, will turn out to be wrong.

But it is another kind of mistake to carry this sort of thing over into public argument. Most citizens will take their first step beyond the conventions only if they think they have an option (as in fact they generally do) about the second step. So the discontent out of which the movement grows needs to be pointed and made precise, and proposed actions need to be described in concrete and limited terms. Neither of these purposes are served by personal descriptions of social crisis or by loose talk, however honest, about the imminent fall of established systems. Sometimes it makes sense to suggest connections between *this* issue and some other, but often not. Sometimes it is useful to sketch out complex aspirations and distant goals, often only to point to near victories. These are political, not personal, decisions, and they depend most of all on a judgment as to the requirements of a particular constituency. I don't mean that activists should lie, only that they should sometimes be silent. Their confessional tendencies especially need to be restrained. Political activity is not a judicial proceeding; activists should tell the truth, but not necessarily the whole of it at every moment.

Symbols

It's not only what we say that is important in politics, but how we look. Visual impacts are sometimes crucial; our appearances signify; they convey meanings to other people. And so it is always necessary for activists to ask: What does this gesture, insignia, costume, flag, mean *to them?* Symbols can be chosen, of course, that mean nothing, to which meanings have to be given—like the bisected circle with an inverted V that has symbolized the peace movement since the 1950's. I don't know what associations that had for its originators; for most of the rest of us, it had none at all. This blankness is probably an advantage: everyone attributes his own significance; no one is turned away.

The clenched fist is a symbol of an exactly opposite sort. It has overwhelming historical associations and in any case carries an immediate and unmistakable meaning. It conveys a sense of aggressiveness and violence which is sometimes intended, but often not, by those who make the gesture. Gestures are like rhetoric: the speaker allows himself to exaggerate, but many members of the audience take him at his word.

Activists rarely reckon with the literal-mindedness of the people in front of whom they act. They think they will be accorded the liberties of the stage even when they are in the streets. Thus obscenity came to be used among some citizen activists at the same time as it came to be used in the theater. But the two uses have very different effects. In the theater, obscenity conveys a shock, a thrill, a sense of danger and extremity (for a little while). But the words themselves don't carry for the audience their literal meaning. In political encounters they do; they express real insult and hostility, and they invite an immediate response which ought never to come as a surprise. The abuse of the flag, as a symbol of political protest, similarly has literal meanings. It is an invitation to patriotic outrage, and that is even worse than personal outrage.

In general, it is a mistake to take one's symbols from the avant-garde culture of the time. To do so inevitably turns political action into an elite performance and a kind of esoteric communication. Similarly, it's a mistake for activists to imitate the life styles of Bohemia—unless it is their primary object to organize Bohemians. Those styles have associations for other people that have or should have nothing to do with movement politics. They represent so much excess weight, and the burdens of dissent are heavy enough. Symbols should lighten the weight, attract new people, make winning easier not harder: V-for-victory is fine.

The presentation of the movement in everyday life does not, at first, appear to be a major problem. When an individual activist canvasses up and down a street, standing in doorways, sitting in living rooms, talking, he is more or less in control of the image he presents. The central committee that directs the canvassing or organizes a demonstration is more or less in control of the immediate impact of those activities. But as soon as a journalist or a cameraman appears on the scene, all such control is lost.

What the media do with the movement is so erratic that it is very difficult to detect a pattern or work out a strategy. Sometimes they pick up a campaign that is struggling along with no great success in sight and publicize it to the nation,

vastly increasing its size and scope. Here is the dream of many
little bands of activists: suddenly to be made important. More
often, the media only glance at citizen politics and reflect the
judgment of the professionals as to its significance. Then
activists think they find a "consistent ideological bias" in
newspaper and television coverage, and they attribute to this
bias the fact that they are being ignored. I suspect they are
wrong (though not always). The consistent bias of the news
media is toward novelty and excitement, not toward right, left,
or center. Of course, what is new today depends on what was
news yesterday. So if one campaign is extensively covered,
the next may not be covered at all; and after a period of
neglect, an activity fitfully sustained for some time will abruptly
be discovered. One does not choose; one is chosen.

Given the essentially arbitrary quality of media coverage,
there is still some room for maneuver. Local newspapers are
especially open: activists able to grind out copy can get
almost as much coverage as they want. And it does matter,
though it is hard to say how much, that press releases be well
written, news conferences properly staged, celebrities and
Great Men intelligently exploited. Political action has or can
have a dramatic quality which activists should not deny or
repress. Nor is it shameful to seek out professional help with
such things, so long as the professionals are told that they
must take the movement as it is, not try to make it more
presentable. (Perhaps the movement *should* be made more
presentable, but that is a political decision and must be made
by the participants themselves.)

There are, however, two dangers to the movement in the media's bias toward novelty and excitement. The first is the danger of rhetorical and tactical escalation in search of publicity. If this activity doesn't attract enough attention, then perhaps this one will, or this one. . . . The inevitable progress is from orderly demonstrations and more or less rational speeches to window-breaking, obscenity, and melodramatic calls for revolution. Steadily over time, the ante is raised, wilder things are said, greater risks accepted. Citizens come to act with one eye on what they are doing, the other fixed on its reflection in the media. They must continually astonish others in order to see themselves.

Amateur activism sometimes is astonishing, and it is always useful for a citizen to make his break with the routines of political life as dramatically as he can. But good politics most often consists in doing the same thing over and over again. Like many other worthwhile human activities, it requires a considerable capacity for boredom. This the media do not encourage, and so their influence must be opposed. The best means of opposition is the development of the movement's internal audience. Hence the need for newsletters, pamphlets, films, aimed at the membership itself and setting standards of political relevance and utility different from those established outside.

The second danger is the overexposure of movement leaders and spokesmen. One of the ways the media produce excitement is by focusing on personality. If no leader has

clearly emerged, or if leadership is shared within the
movement, the most colorful figure will be sought out and
designated Prince. He will be filmed and interviewed endlessly,
his opinions asked on a dozen different subjects, each of his
performances edited so as to single out his most extravagant
words and gestures, his most "interesting" self. It may be
that he doesn't have opinions on a dozen different subjects,
that his extravagant words represent no one else's views: it
doesn't matter. Nor will he find it easy to resist the temptations
of sudden fame. The movement, after all, needs publicity; if
he can be its agent, has he any right to refuse the opportunity?

There are three victims here: the media audience which is
entertained but not informed; the movement membership
which is misrepresented; and the media Prince himself, who is
all too quickly used up. He may be an exciting man, but if he
keeps talking he won't be exciting for long: soon enough,
someone else will be discovered. And meanwhile, other
activists who trusted him as one of themselves suddenly see
him in a new light: Who is he to speak so loudly? The
instability of leadership among citizen activists is at least
partly explicable in these terms. A man hardly has time to
build a firm political base before he receives national publicity
and is ruthlessly exposed to the (suspicious) eyes of his
associates and followers. What can he do? Above all, he must
refuse to join in the games to which he is incessantly invited,
the game of *épater le bourgeois,* the game of maximal leader,
the game of instant opinion. He must reflect views widely held,
even if he states them in his own fashion and with his own

emphasis; he must drag other people into the limelight with him; he must master the techniques of evasion and refusal.

It makes little sense, however, to refuse absolutely to face a camera or talk to a journalist. This is sometimes seen as the path of integrity. We will keep control of our own faces, activists say, and present only our unmediated selves to the world. The political purposes of the movement make that an impossible decision. One can't refuse to be described, discussed, reported. The activist has chosen to seek public effects, to influence other people, to change (some part of) their lives. He not only needs publicity; *they* deserve that his actions be publicized. So he has a public face, willy-nilly, and that inevitably means a face he can't entirely control. As a result, of course, he is not entirely responsible for his appearance. But he must take responsibility and do the best he can.

There are only a limited number of things to do, so it is important, first, to do them well and, second, to do them enough. Movement debates about tactics, however, rarely focus on these two imperatives. They are often disguised arguments about leaders, issues, strategies, organizational structures. And it does make sense, at least sometimes, to avoid the larger questions until they are forcibly raised by the pressures of day-to-day activity and the need for (what look like) tactical decisions. But activists should always be aware of exactly what is being decided. If canvassing is organized by ward and precinct, a future electoral campaign is being set up (and if not, not); if every local group is authorized to bring its own signs to the demonstration, a federal and,

possibly, multi-issue movement is being established, and
so on.

But tactics have also an interest and value of their own.
Leaders and movements survive, after all, largely on tactical
successes. Day after day, they must find things to do, from
which activists will carry away a sense of meaning and effect
and which other people also will notice and remember. What
sorts of things?

Canvassing

This is the most natural form of movement politics. Citizens
talk to citizens, free for a time of the interferences of the
political system and the mass media. It is most effective if the
canvassers are neighbors or near neighbors, working in an
area they know well. They should canvass, if possible, in
groups of two, and since they will often be visiting homes
where the man is away, at least one of the two should be a
woman. They should be trained to avoid anger and
recrimination and discouraged from involving themselves in
long arguments. Argument is a most dangerous kind of self-
indulgence. Canvassers come away often enough certain that
they have won a major intellectual victory and left a convert.
But the effect of such easy victories is usually just the opposite.
Canvassing should aim at nothing more than making people
aware of the movement and its issue, finding those who are
already in agreement, and opening up the others to future
persuasion. No one is likely to be turned around in an hour or

a day, and to try to turn people around so quickly only suggests the arrogance of the committed.

Canvassers need a reason for coming to people's doors beyond the issue itself, and they sometimes want a reason for coming back. They can carry a petition or distribute a leaflet or publicize a meeting. When they find sympathizers, they should try to get them together for block or neighborhood discussions—at which a movement spokesman can be present. Most often, probably, they will be urging people to vote one way or another on a referendum statement, a candidate, or a party. Then the canvass must also serve as a poll, so that movement leaders will know where they are strong and where not. It is especially important that accurate records be kept of each encounter with a potential voter.

The value of electoral canvassing is much disputed. Clearly, it is or can be effective in getting out a large vote, but if the canvassers are working in unfriendly territory, their work may be no great gain—it may even be a real loss—for the cause. So electoral canvassing must often be limited to the movement's own constituency: it is simply a means of alerting sympathetic people to the importance of a particular campaign. It serves no other purpose; it does not extend the constituency, introduce new people to the cause, build the movement. It may not even have the effect of convincing sympathetic people of the "right" political position, since canvassers are likely to be limited in what they can say by the not-quite-satisfactory position of their candidate. Nevertheless, these are limitations worth living with, given a

reasonable chance of winning the election. For victory builds
the movement and extends its range faster than the most
energetic and zealous canvass.

Demonstrating

This is the easiest activity. It requires nothing more than that
supporters of the cause get together. They must get together,
however, in large enough numbers to demonstrate strength
and not weakness. Demonstrations have two purposes, both
of which are best served and possibly only served by numbers.
They rally the activists, firing them for future work. They
impress the general population, but especially its political
leaders, with the power, passion, social range, respectability,
or whatever of the movement.

There is always disagreement, of course, over just what ought
to be demonstrated to or impressed upon the general
population. A really massive demonstration is likely to require
the support of a variety of political groups—sects and parties
and independent locals as well as the single-issue movement
itself. Perhaps the demonstration is organized by a coalition
committee whose different members have quite different
purposes in mind. Some way must be found, however, to
establish a common discipline and a single official line, a list
of speakers at the rally and spokesmen for the cause. And
here the single-issue movement, assuming some minimal
resourcefulness among its leaders, is by far the most likely
group to win out. For it is very difficult, whatever signs or
leaflets or speakers say, to demonstrate for more than one
thing at a time. All sorts of arguments may be put forward at

a demonstration for nuclear disarmament, say, or against this
or that foreign war; the most complex ideological positions
may be presented, the most provocative slogans shouted. If
the occasion is right and the event itself minimally organized,
all that will be remembered is that so many people turned out
for nuclear disarmament or against the war.

But I don't want to suggest that signs, leaflets, and speakers
are unimportant. The more complete the discipline the
movement can impose, the more effective the demonstration
—for the movement (and, presumably, for the cause). Only if
the movement is or appears to be in control will professional
politicians want to work with its leaders, seek their
endorsement, support their political position. No one wants or
needs to work with a coalition committee that doesn't even
try to control its followers in any systematic way. Politicians
will appeal over the heads of such a group, directly to the
mass of sympathizers and activists. And these people will
respond on their own, rather than as an organized
constituency.

Efforts are usually made to locate demonstrations at some
central point: the capital or largest city. This is obviously
worth doing, but not always. A word should be said for the
local demonstration. It is one of the strengths of citizen politics
that it often creates significant local bases here and there
throughout the country, where its part-time activists live and
work full time. This is an achievement that is sometimes worth
revealing, making public in some striking way. Rootedness is
an impressive political fact. But the people who troop across

the country for a rally in Washington or New York often look like marginal people. National demonstrations attract *demonstrators;* local demonstrations attract citizens. It is much harder, of course, to get activists to rally or march in front of their friends and neighbors, but efforts should certainly be made to persuade them to do so. The election eve parade and bonfire is a bit of old-fashioned politicking that the movement might well revive.

Planning a demonstration always involves negotiation with the police. So long as the police are willing to permit an activity more or less of the sort the movement leadership wants or hopes for, it is obviously wisest to reach agreement with them on all necessary details. Refusal by the police (or by their political superiors) may be made an occasion for disobedience, in the name of civil liberty or of the cause itself. This is an important political decision, however, and it should hang on political factors. Perhaps the most crucial of these is the kind of discipline movement leaders believe they can impose on their followers. If they have no confidence in their own authority, they probably should not challenge that of the police. A general melee most often tends to enhance the civil power, the forces of "law and order," and may lead to the repression of the movement. It will almost certainly lead to the hasty retreat of many citizen activists who had not bargained for that sort of thing at all. I suppose there are or will be occasions when such risks are worth taking, but no one should doubt the magnitude of the risks.

Demonstrations don't always require large numbers of people.

They can produce effects in two other ways: when the people involved, though only a few, are already well known; and when they do surprising or dangerous or illegal things. To get a few prominent men and women to march across the city, picket a government building, or break the law in some demonstrative fashion sometimes lies within the power of the movement and is sometimes useful. For the rest, these are acts of witness, personal choices, and not tactical decisions.

Striking and Boycotting

These are efforts to exercise power as well as to demonstrate it, and the exercise must be effective or it is meaningless. Virtually every activist dreams at least once in his political life of winning through a general strike—the whole society (or the working class), one great rally for the cause! But except within the labor movement, even much more limited strikes are not likely options. Movement constituencies are rarely large enough, or socially located in the right way, to pull off a strike, and movement discipline is rarely tough enough to maintain it. Citizen activists will often resent claims on them that go beyond the time they have contributed. They try (not always) to keep their work lives and their family lives apart from their politics, and this is an attempt that has to be respected, even if movement leaders hope one day to involve them further. Boycotts are easier precisely because they make such minimal demands on participants.

Tax refusal and draft resistance are both forms of strikes; at least, they are so intended. I don't believe that either has ever had the desired coercive effects, for no political movement

has ever been able to mobilize a large enough constituency
to carry them off as strikes. But the refusal or resistance of a
few people who personally accept the risks involved may be
an impressive demonstration of feeling and commitment,
inspiring other activists to lesser sorts of opposition. Here a
great deal depends, obviously, on the public demeanor (and
the public relations) of the resisters and refusers.

Electioneering

At some point the movement will almost certainly come to this,
and should, with whatever misgivings. The referendum is its
most obvious electoral recourse, for here it can carry its single
issue directly to the mass of voters and run a "pure"
campaign, unlikely to disturb its most committed members.
New voters can be registered who may be useful later on. And
since many citizens who won't do anything else for the cause
will vote for it and even do routine election work, an
organization can be built on the ward and precinct level. The
independent, single-issue candidate is another easy choice.
He is unlikely to win, but his campaign can serve to spread the
word, and a good vote can have significant demonstration
effects. (As I have already indicated, these are not entirely
compatible goals.) A single-issue campaign may also put
considerable pressure on one of the major parties to make
the cause its own and so win the support of whatever
constituency is being mobilized.

As soon as a major party does this, the movement is involved,
whether it chooses to be or not, in a conventional election.
It need not, however, become the mere captive of the party

that adopts its cause. Now every tactical maneuver becomes important if the movement is to retain its own identity and its organizational integrity. It is especially vital that some way be found to keep control of the canvassing operation out of the hands of party regulars. The election itself may be victory enough for them, but it is at best only the next-to-last step for the movement.

All these tactics, and others too, can be employed as parts of different strategies. They can be combined in a great variety of ways, carried on simultaneously or sequentially. It is only important to remember that no one of them is in any simple sense the right thing to do; no one of them promises final victory. For this reason, tactical choices should always have two characteristics: they should be repeatable (in the way that a *Kamikaze* pilot's attack is not); and they should not have to be repeated, that is, they should not lock the movement into a particular kind of politics. Activists must always be prepared to do the same thing again and again, and be no less prepared to do something else next.

The plural form is important. Activist citizens rarely if ever confront a single opponent, a unified hierarchy of professional politicians and bureaucrats, or an all-powerful Establishment —any more than any of these confront a conspiracy of citizens. It is easier to take aim if one resolutely disbelieves in plurality, but much harder to score a hit. In fact, the movement, whatever its character, faces a variety of enemies, who usually have considerable difficulty coordinating their resistance. They are inhibited by old rivalries, or they disagree, much as activists do, about strategy and tactics, or they see a chance for a little easy blackmail. It might be that all of them would band together if the movement posed a truly major threat. But even the history of revolutionary struggle does not reveal that kind of unity, and, in any case, the

movement does not often pose an equally major threat to all
established groups. Indeed, it sometimes offers opportunities,
above all, to leading politicians, who have often been known
to desert their traditional allies (aristocrats, bishops,
landowners, industrialists, managers) in exchange for mass
support.

Instead of presupposing enmity, on the basis of this or that
ideological vision, activists must always be on the lookout
for secret allies. Because the conventional system is itself
competitive, every intervention is bound to have different
effects on groups differently situated within it, on parties and
individuals, for example, in and out of office. A massive
demonstration may discredit the mayor or governor and win
private applause from an opposition that would never organize
demonstrations. A referendum campaign may increase the
size of the election-day poll and help whatever party draws
support from passive majorities. A growing movement is itself
a candidate for alliances and coalitions undreamt of by its
militants. These are not stable ties, to be sure, but they
should never be spurned before the possibilities they open
are carefully studied.

No one should be called an enemy until he has earned the
title. Movement leaders, of course, must calculate their
chances of winning support here or there in the society as
realistically as they can. But their public stance should be
open as long as openness is at all safe. They need to win
support from people whose first response is worried, unsure,
or hostile, and they can only do that if they avoid labeling those

people on the basis of their first response. Some enemies are implacable, but that is no reason to set out to make implacable enemies.

Even if it does not seek out enemies, however, a movement may find itself fundamentally at odds with conventional moral or political standards, or with established social interests. Then it is forced to make the best of its embattled state, and since its every action is an affront or a threat to large numbers of men and women, the available options are limited. It is a great temptation, at such moments, to blame the people who are affronted and threatened. Who else is responsible for the isolation and failure of the movement? But just as seventeenth-century pamphleteers always attacked not the king but the king's advisers, so today one must attack not the people but the people's leaders. For the rest, the tasks of an isolated band of activists are obviously educational: it must put its case, doing whatever is necessary to attract some notice, but never insulting those who turn away unconvinced. It must look and sound more winning than it is.

First they worked within the system, and failed; then they
moved outside: this is a typical activist's description of
extra-legal militancy. Short of revolution, however, it is not
so easy to move outside. Even extra-legal actions must aim
at producing effects within the system; there is no other
place where effects can be had. So militant tactics must
always be calculated in systematic terms. The necessary
questions are obvious ones: What kind of support will they
build? What kind of pressure will they put on conventional
politicians? I am not going to consider here the moral
implications of such questions. It is enough to point out that
the commitment of activists to act as effectively as they can
for the cause *is* a moral commitment. They have no right to
harm their own cause, and so they must resist the pressures

of personal frustration and anger that so often lead them to do so. Their calculations must be dispassionate and impersonal. These qualities are more likely the functions of organizational discipline than moral exhortation, but that only suggests the moral value of organizational discipline.

There are times when extra-legal action serves the cause. The clearest cases are those in which citizen activists already have widespread but latent support, and when all that is required for victory is the acting out of systemic values. But mass inertia, particular interests, the obstacle course of routine politics all stand in the way. Then it may well be helpful if some significant number of citizens breaks the law in order to demonstrate the importance (to them) of their cause. They say to their fellow citizens: if you don't do this or that, which you know ought to be done, you will have to put us in prison. Such demonstrations work, or sometimes work, precisely because they call attention to some common knowledge of what is right and good. Thus the history of the extension of suffrage to workers, women, and blacks: extra-legal action was effective in large part because no one watching it had good reasons (I mean, reasons they were confident about) to deny the justice of the cause. And so they were unwilling or morally unable to support a sustained program of repression and punishment directed against the activists.

When activists do confront sustained repression (as has happened often in the history of the labor movement), another kind of law-breaking may be necessary. Sometimes it is not possible to act at all, or to act with any hope of success, without setting oneself against laws (or executive orders, court injunctions, police commands) that aim explicitly at preventing collective action. Then activists break the law for the sake of reaching and mobilizing their own constituency and without any immediate reference to wider effects. Even here, however, it is wisest to act within limits, for the possibility of influencing other people should never be entirely forgotten.

People are not favorably influenced by being assaulted. Doubtless they can be forced to act in some new or different way, and if politics comes to that (to war and revolution), then one wants one's assaults to be massive. But given the hope of systemic effects, of repealing this law or changing that policy, even, simply, of ongoing political work, persuasion must be considerably more delicate. The need for caution and limit is especially urgent in the absence of common values. Then the almost certain effect of extra-legal action, and above all of violence, is to increase the distance between the band of activists and everyone else. Not only is the movement proposing new policies which many people don't understand and which they fear, but its members are pressing their proposals, acting every day, willfully and publicly, in incomprehensible and frightening ways. They may think they have moved outside the system, but in fact they have only set themselves up to be driven out. They will be driven, most likely, into sectarian isolation, where many of them will in time discover they don't want to be.

I ought to mention one further use of militance by citizen

activists: they sometimes point to the violence or the threatened violence *of others* as a warning to society as a whole. There, they say to their fellow citizens, but for your acquiescence or support, go we. This is really a cry for help rather than a threat on their own part (and if a threat, not always a serious one). Like the boy's cry of "Wolf!" it can't be said too often. But there are occasions when citizen politics is only one of many possible responses to a crisis and when the others, or some of them, are dangerous to the political system (or, more often, simply to life and limb). Then the warning is plausible and may even be heeded; certainly it is worth making—soberly and quietly, if possible, as by Martin Luther King in the early 1960's. I need hardly say that it is not possible to work out in advance a division of labor between violent militants and citizen activists, so that the second group draws advantages from the outrages of the first. Nor should the activists ever pretend that if they win concessions, they can call off the militants.

Sectarianism is the dead end of party politics within the movement. At the same time, it is a way of surviving at the dead end—even surviving for a long time—and this gives it a certain attraction.

Initially, some of the activists work out or seek out an ideology to help explain to themselves what they are doing, and why. They hold their new beliefs tentatively; they bear them lightly within the movement, cooperating with other men and women who do not share them. But then the movement suffers defeats or fails to win victories, and its participants begin to question their easy camaraderie: doesn't it conceal a refusal to face up to difficult choices, to plan for the long haul? Here is an ideology, some of them say, that describes the long haul and accounts also for our short-term setbacks, placing the movement squarely within a progressive history. Surely everyone must adopt this ideology and guide their activities in accordance with its picture of the world.

Everyone, of course, does not agree, but those who do cling more and more closely together. They begin to meet separately, distinguishing one another from the rest of the movement by their intimately shared knowledge of ideological detail. They spend much of their time testing one another, and at moments of internal crisis denouncing, purging, splitting from one another. Their willful isolation brings with it further political defeats. For each of these there is an ideological explanation. Gradually, the explanatory system becomes total, self-contained, proof against all the vicissitudes of experience. It ceases to be a way of knowing the world and becomes instead a protection against it, a hard shell within which the intense but limited life of a political sect is carried on. While the movement may well win and fade away, the sect loses and survives.

This is a model history. Obviously, it is possible to arrive at the same dead end by different routes. And along any of these there will be stopping points short of perfect sectarian isolation. Sometimes the leaders of citizen movements, clubs, or parties will even seek out some such stopping point because it offers the hope of permanence and stability, if only on the margins of the conventional political world. I mean, it establishes a political base by sacrificing something of the momentum of the movement, its thrust toward short-term resolutions of single issues. This may be a self-serving choice, but it's not necessarily that. There are important political purposes that can be served by the existence of a marginal party or a political club, like the Liberals or the Reform Democrats in New York. They can develop and try out proposals that one or another of the major parties might one day adopt; they can shift the parties (slightly) this way or that; they can reach into and mobilize sectors of society that the major parties cannot reach, and so on. In any case, survival is always a great temptation.

But what is the political purpose of surviving as a sect? It's not an accident that the word "sect" comes to us from religious history. The survival of religious sects makes sense, for they claim to fix their members in a proper relation to God. And that relation is an end in itself, a value that needn't be referred to the experience of other people. It might be better if the others shared in the relation, but better only for them. The sect member has already achieved his most important desire. This is obviously not so in a political sect. Its internal life may be marvelously vivid and intense, but it is not self-redeeming unless it redeems the others.

What often happens, however, is that the internal life of the sect becomes a substitute for all external effects. I don't mean that sectarian militants don't seek external effects. Their ideology teaches them, most likely, that they will have further opportunities to change the world, if only they cling together now and hold fast to the truths they share. Indeed, there are further opportunities, and the remnants of the last movement participate in the next. Sometimes they are able to do so in helpful ways, adopting the strategy known on the Left as the "united front," and cooperating as honestly as they can with people who don't share their faith. More often, I am afraid, they participate in the movement only in order to recruit new members for their own internal life. They have lost the commitment to single issues, the tactical flexibility, the taste for small victories—all the essential characteristics of citizen politics. They anticipate defeat and are carriers of defeat, and that is why their influence within the movement almost always has to be resisted.

Winning and Losing

24

It is best to win. It is also best to appear to be winning, and since the movement is involved in an ongoing series of activities, it is usually possible to plan for a series of successes. These will mostly be small triumphs, and triumphs, perhaps, only by the movement's own measure: a successful rally, a march larger than the last march, more names on a petition than anyone expected (expectations should be low), this or that conventional politician turning around, agreeing to speak, looking for support. Such victories make the growth of the movement apparent, and movements grow, in fact, by appearing to grow. Hence the importance of the demonstration and the sequence of demonstrations, which must be aimed, above all, at communicating a sense of expansion, of numerical increase and greater social range.

There is always pressure among the activists, however, to escalate rather than expand; that is, to heighten the militancy of successive demonstrations, revealing to the country the increasing zealousness of (a part of) the movement. But escalation of this sort almost always decreases the numerical strength and narrows the social range of political action, often in disastrously sudden ways. It may even be better, though psychologically much more difficult, to move in the other direction: to lower the level of militancy over time in order to maximize growth. In any case, one appears to be winning, and one actually wins, only by reaching and involving more and more people.

It is possible to survive minor defeats, but it isn't always desirable to survive a whole series of minor defeats. If sectarian isolation is the only recourse, it is probably best to dissolve altogether and, assuming the continued significance of the cause, let some new group of people come together, differently organized, differently led, to carry on the struggle. The history of a political cause often takes this form: a number of organizations and movements, rising and falling, peaking at different points, some of them collapsing and vanishing. Only after a long time does one or another achieve enough strength to win. A history of this sort is possible because citizen activists have other things to do (other causes to work for). The movement isn't the whole of their lives, nor should it be. Activists should remember this too: they have worked hard; they can (sometimes) withdraw from the field with honor. Their part-time activity is not indispensable to the cause; the cause is not indispensable to their own lives. When a new

start is necessary, it isn't or shouldn't be difficult to clear
the way.

Major defeats are often caused by reaching too soon for
major victories. But judgments about timing are among the
most difficult of political choices. The succession of minor
triumphs can't be sustained indefinitely, even by the most
skillful tactician. In any case, the impatience of the activists,
the demand for more decisive action, greater risks, total
victory, will grow over time. Here one can only weigh internal
pressure for one or another culmination against the external
possibilities of achieving it. Leaders who stake everything on
sudden victory are likely to be replaced, if they don't destroy
the movement altogether, by leaders who lower the stakes.
Those who keep the stakes too low too long are likely to be
replaced by gamblers and adventurers.

Victory brings problems too. Ideally, the movement should
simply dissolve, with some of its members retiring to private
life, others moving on to the next cause. But victories are
rarely total, and it is not always certain that they can be
sustained. Then some effort must be made to hold the
constituency together, to institutionalize the movement as a
lobby or pressure group, to establish a foothold in the world
of routine politics. This is going to look like selling out to a
great many movement members. Indeed, any acceptance of
victory may look like that, for activists always turn out to have
hoped for more than victory brings. But it is hard to figure out
a way of winning that does not involve surrendering the

excitements and aspirations of fighting. And, assuming again the importance of the issue that first brought the movement together, it is better to win. There is always another fight.

A Call to
Political Action

I wrote in an earlier chapter that political life is different in different geographic and social locations, in different parts of the country, in different parts of the city. It also changes, obviously, from one historical moment to another. Politics is sometimes interesting, urgent, dangerous; more often, in any decent society, it is none of those things. The judgments we make of these different moments are bound to be ambiguous, and not only because some people flourish amidst urgency and danger, while others feel the full impact of the old Chinese curse: May you live in interesting times! A quiet and routine politics often conceals injustice and oppression, while "interesting times" are moments not only of risk but also of opportunity—for mobilization, revolt, social change. And citizen politics is one of the most important ways in which opportunity can be seized.

We are cursed and blessed with "interesting times." The struggle for racial equality and the struggle against the Vietnam War have mobilized large numbers of previously passive citizens, but they have also sharply divided the country, strained its political institutions, generated sporadic and increasingly serious violence. Doubtless the causes for all this lie deeper than the immediate issues suggest, though it is difficult to overestimate the extent to which the Vietnam War especially is a national disaster (and a disaster perpetrated, it should be remembered, by professionals and experts). But that is not the whole story of our troubles. The political moments of peace and equality have coincided with a more profound crisis.

In the United States today, a society whose government and economy have been progressively removed from the effective control of its citizens, or whose citizens feel themselves to be powerless and disorganized, suddenly faces a series of revolts. These are spurred by real injustices, but are not necessarily dependent on injustice for their energy and force. Very often the revolts don't have an obvious terminating point or a clear political character. Reflecting as much the general crisis as the concrete necessities of any particular cause, citizen politics has taken on the most inchoate forms, failing to achieve either national leadership or collective discipline, generating a kind of random militancy. The causes

for which activists are recruited are not always the reasons,
or the most important reasons, for their activities.

Nothing has a more disorienting effect upon political action
than the sense of powerlessness—except, perhaps,
powerlessness itself. It produces what might best be called
political promiscuity, a feeling that anything goes, a desperate
search for immediate if superficial effects because real effects
are by definition beyond reach. And since the most desirable
immediate effects are those of extremity and outrage, it
produces at the same time a steady escalation toward
revolutionary struggle (or, at least, revolutionary rhetoric)—
as if powerlessness, which can't be overcome by increments
and stages, might be transformed in one unexpected stroke.
This whole style of citizen activism appeals most of all, I think,
to new activists, whose escape from one or another passive
role is most recent and whose sense of political possibility is
barely developed. It does not serve the cause, whatever the
cause is: instead, it invites the defeat and repression for which
it is also a subtle kind of psychic preparation. What can the
powerless hope for except defeat?

Citizen politics is not easy in the United States today; it would
be foolish to pretend that it is, or to hold before the eyes of
new activists the formal model of a democratic system. In
almost every area of social life they are certain to encounter
entrenched and efficient bureaucracies which evade, resist,
wear down, or simply absorb the force of their protest. The
decline of political parties and of legislative authority has
clearly reduced the accessibility of the political system and

made the work of newly activated citizens much harder than
it once was. Nevertheless, there is abundant evidence to
suggest that access is still possible and that bureaucracies
can be pushed this way or that (even when they can't be
seized and transformed).

A citizens' movement, carefully organized, intelligently led,
can win important victories, on both the local and national
levels, short of Total Victory. Both the civil rights and Black
Power movements of the 1960's, and the peace movement
too, had significant effects on American politics. They reached
new constituencies, forced professional politicians to pay
attention, built up local power bases, won changes in
executive policies and bureaucratic procedures. These
(small) victories ought to have been more heartening than
they were, and might have been followed up in more
successful ways, had there existed a larger number of activists
scornful of apocalyptic talk and ready for the risks and
sacrifices of an ongoing politics.

What would that look like? Why is that so hard? It requires
self-control and organizational discipline, for one thing, and
then the acting out of the kind of politics I have tried to
describe, where every step is measured and pleasure is
rarely immediate or ecstatic. It requires activists to live with
and make compromises with men and women whose opinions
they abhor, for no other reason than that these men and
women are (temporarily perhaps) more powerful, or more
numerous, or simply because they are *there*. An ongoing
politics is not one whose participants can possibly hope to

deliver "all power to the people" tomorrow or next month. For they represent only some of the people and must hope to win what they can win: a little more power for this or that newly organized group. And that is only possible if they work at it long and hard enough. . . .

Right now it is important to work at it long and hard. The causes for the sake of which so many of us enlisted are serious enough, but the dangers of defeat once the battle has been joined, as it has been joined in the United States today, are more serious still. It has been joined, in part, by young militants without a community base or a coherent strategy; by sectarian ideologues even more out of touch but with an all-too-coherent strategy; by isolated terrorists insanely committed to the efficacy of The Act, responsible to no one. Without the long-term activism of adult citizens, the central political movements of our time belong to them. And there is nothing more certain than that the revolution of their heated fantasies will end in a brutal and squalid repression, a bitter defeat not only for them.

The militants, sectarians, and terrorists regard themselves as the vanguard of the people; perhaps so, but they are a lost vanguard, and it is not even remotely likely that the people, whoever they are, will follow. The real question is whether citizen activists can find another way. Surely there are many thousands of Americans who will join them if they can, forging a political movement that is committed but also sane and steady in the pursuit of its goals and that makes itself an instrument as well as a symbol of democratic possibility. Nor is there any reason to think that these Americans are less fervent than those who have marched away with the lost vanguard. They are, perhaps, more modest—as befits participants in a citizens' movement. And many of them probably look forward to a time when political action is not so urgent as it is today. They are not the sort of people who will ever win glory. *But no one else can carry us forward to a society less oppressive, less unjust, more routinely democratic than the one we have now.*

A Note on the Author

Michael Walzer is Professor of Government at Harvard University, though, as he is quick to note, "this book reflects my own experience in civil rights and anti-war politics—rather than my experience as a professor of political science." Born in New York City in 1935, Mr. Walzer studied at Brandeis, at Cambridge University, England (as a Fulbright Scholar), and at Harvard. He is the author of *The Revolution of the Saints: A Study in the Origins of Radical Politics* and *Obligations: Essays on Disobedience, War, and Citizenship,* and editor (with Philip Green) of *The Political Imagination in Literature.*